Fiction
Writing
DEMYSTIFIED

Fiction Writing

DEMYSTIFIED

Techniques That *Will* Make *You* a More Successful Writer

By Thomas B. Sawyer

ASHLEYWILDE™ INC

FICTION WRITING DEMYSTIFIED

Techniques That *Will* Make
You a More Successful Writer

Published by Ashleywilde, Inc.

For information, address:
Ashleywilde, Inc.
23852 Pacific Coast Highway, #132
Malibu, California 90265
www.ashleywilde.com

ISBN 0-9627476-1-0
Library of Congress Control Number: 2002110026

Printed in the United States of America

Design and production
Leena Hannonen, Macnetic Design

For Holly, and my parents.

ACKNOWLEDGEMENTS

My thanks to all those seasoned writers who held my hand in the months and years following my discovery of my calling. My gratitude also to Dr. Sidney Levy, and to Leonard Starr, mentor, friend, brother, without whose guidance none of this could have happened. And especially, I thank my parents for endowing me with so many assets, perhaps the most valuable being a lifetime supply of chutzpah and blanket invulnerability to rejection.

Contents

Acknowledgements   **vii**

Preface

An Approach to Storytelling   xv

ONE – The Writer's Mindset   **1**

Face it – We're *Entertainers*   1

The TV Writer's Mandate   2

The TV Writer's Bogeyman   3

The Hitchcock Motto   4

The Computer in Your Head   6

Write to The Money   7

TWO – Beginnings – The Story *Idea*   **9**

Asking Yourself "Where's The Heat?"   9

A Word or Two About Originality   10

Stealing Stories From Oneself   14

Predictability   15

The Story *Idea*   16

Pitching   18

THREE – The Process   **27**

Building Your Story   27

What *is* a Story Outline and How does it Differ

    From a Synopsis or a Treatment?   30

What Does a Story Outline *Look* Like?   31

One More Plea (But *Not* the Last)

    On Behalf of Outlining – Or –

    How the "Drudgery" of Writing Your Outline

    Will Turn Into Pleasure   32

Conflict Defined   33

About Texture   35

Red Flags   36

Play the Moments – Don't Just Talk About Them   39

The Money Scene   44

The Plot Device   46

Clock   47

Maguffins   47

Hiding in Plain Sight   48

Meet-Cute   48

Platforming   49

The Deus Ex Machina   50

Parallel Action   51

The Penny-Drop   51

Coincidence   52

Sounds   53

The Moral Decision   54

Using Research – Without Letting it Use *You*   55

Closure   56

Let Your Characters Generate Their *Own* Stories   57

FOUR – Creating Vivid, Memorable,

Engaging Characters **59**

Start With the _Edges_ 59

Avoid Flat-Out Opposites 63

Find the Facets 63

Thrust 65

Goals – Small and Large 67

Make it Worth Your Characters'

Time – _and_ it'll be Worth Your Audience's 68

Franchises 69

The Character Bio 75

Attitudes and Conditions 79

The TV Series Character-Mix 82

Naming Your Characters 85

Give 'em Secrets 87

Liars Play Better Than Saints 89

Habits, Hang-ups, Hobbies and Hatreds 91

Find the _Permutations_ of Conflict 92

Character-types: More About Heroines and Heroes 93

Make Your Audience _Cheer_ For Your Protagonist 94

The Fatally Flawed Protagonist 94

Attractive Protagonists 97

Intriguing Heavies 99

Outsiders 105

Con-Artists and Other Appealing Rascals 106

Character Arcs 108

Remember, They Had Lives _Before_ Page One 109

Discovering, and Then _Listening_ to Your Characters 110

Character Traps 114

Making *All* of Your Characters *Count*   116

Some Characterization House-Numbers   117

Anger   117

Passive-Aggressive   118

Control   118

Hunger for Approval   119

Caretaker   120

Low Self-Esteem   120

Psychopaths and Sociopaths   120

The *Really* Hard Part – Or – What *Should* Be The
    Hardest Part: Introducing Your Characters to
    Your Audience   124

Exposition   128

Don't tell it. *Show* it!   128

Amateur Exposition – The Dreaded "*But, you
    <u>are</u> my sister…*" Syndrome, and Other Sins   128

Front-loading – Some Advice – and Some Solutions   130

FIVE – Construction – *Telling* Your Story   133

Plotting – Laying Out Your Story   133

Plot Conveniences, Holes, and Other
    Audience Distractions   137

Plugging Plot Holes   139

How to Get Ahead of Your
    Audience – and Stay There   141

Knowing What to Include – and
    What to Leave Out   145

Backstory   147

Playing Fair   148

Point-of-View 149

Focus 151

Scene Structure 152

Choreography 153

THINK Picture/THINK Action/THINK
Dialogue – A Screenwriter's Approach 155

Stoppers 157

More About Where to Start a Scene and Where to
End it – Or – Why the Playwright's Curse is
the Novelist's and Screenwriter's Blessing 158

Punchlines, Buttons and Act-Outs 160

The *Non-Scene* – Causes and Cures 162

Kicking It Off – That *Super*-Critical
Opening Moment 164

Payoffs and Blowoffs – The Endgame – Or –
More Fastballs and Curves 164

SIX – Writing Great, *Unique* Dialogue **171**

"*Unique* Dialogue" Defined 171

Self-Explainers (and Other Works of Fiction) 172

Hearing Your Characters' Music 174

Subtext 175

Functional Dialogue – and How to Avoid It 176

Listen to the *Silences* 176

Helping *Direct* Your Actors' Dialogue 179

Memorable Dialogue 179

Dialect 180

Crosstalk 181

The Aria 181

Staying *With* It   182

Tombstoning   183

Don't Tell Your Audience What It Already Knows   183

NEVER Write Show-and-Tell Dialogue   185

Energy/Urgency   185

Dialogue Attribution in Prose – An Opinion or Two...   189

SEVEN – Coda   **191**

The Rorschach View   191

INDEX   **197**

PREFACE

An Approach to Storytelling

During 20 years as a writer/producer or story editor on 16 different network TV series, my experience has been dramatically different from that of most working fiction writers. In addition to writing my own scripts, I listened to hundreds of story-pitches from both staffers and freelancers, generated and commissioned hundreds of scripts which I then oversaw and edited. Of necessity, a large part of my job has been that of teacher.

But *not* a teacher of theory.

Rather, of *nuggets* about writing — of *explaining* to other writers – and to myself in the bargain – in clear, concise language, very specific, problem-solving ways to improve the end product.

Where it *misses*. How to *fix* it. To make it *work* better.

It is not entirely surprising that *many* of the rather specialized, highly pragmatic techniques one learns in the pressure-driven world of writing for series TV translate readily to fiction writing of *any* kind, from short stories to novels to stageplays to movie scripts. Even, for that matter, to poetry, non-fiction – such as biography – and textbooks.

What *is* surprising is that this practical, result-oriented approach is seldom featured in books on writing or in creative writing courses. Touched on, perhaps, but *not* in the kind of depth that makes it all of a piece. One possible reason is that many of the books are written, and courses taught, by writers who, if they've *had* professional writing careers, have, like the majority of their fellows understandably spent much of their creative lives sitting in rooms by themselves, living mostly inside their heads. *Thinking* about what they're writing rather than talking about it — rather than *needing* to analyze it in order to explain to others what they do — and *why* they're doing it a particular way.

Rather than – as in my own case – being paid to show *other working writers* how to solve their manuscript problems.

That's why I wrote this book, to help spell out, make accessible, to *demystify* those aspects and methods of storytelling that may seem daunting – or even unknowable – to so many would-be writers. For them, and for those who may already have many of the bits and pieces of storytelling knowledge rattling about willy-nilly in their brains, I hope that reading these pages will help organize – and again, de-intimidate them.

That is what this book is about.

I haven't invented anything new about storytelling or characterization or construction. I certainly don't claim to know *everything* there is to know about fiction writing – as *if* that were possible. I continue to learn, and to be amazed by the process of writing. You won't necessarily find anything here that isn't covered in other books or courses in creative writing — or that you're not familiar with on some level. But because of those peculiar demands of my career, of having *had* to find fresh ways of looking at stories (my own as well as others'), to *quickly* nail the stuff that doesn't work, *and* improve the stuff that does, much about the craft has become clearer to me.

Including the fact that good, effective, workmanlike fiction writing does not demand genius.

But — it's not something *everyone* can do.

It requires talent. Which you probably possess to some degree or you wouldn't be reading this; the desire to create usually — not always, but usually — presupposes that you have *some* gift for the art.

And, writing fiction takes *knowledge* about basic storytelling. Again, some of us have an instinct for it. A feeling for it. But if you sense that you do not, don't give up. Much of that part is craft, and it is learnable. In my own case, as I'm sure it was (is) for many of you, when I began writing in earnest I discovered to my surprise that I *knew* more than I thought I did. And the knowledge seemed to amount to more than just an awareness of the differences between good writing and bad writing. I have the impression, from my travels as a guest-speaker on the Writer's Conference Circuit, and my experience as a teacher of screenwriting, that this is a common phenomenon. The result, I suspect, of our almost universal, close-to-saturation exposure – by the time we reach adulthood — to *stories*, of our having read or viewed or otherwise absorbed hundreds or even thousands of them — from the classic children's tales to countless episodes of *I Love Lucy* and other shows, to movies, novels and so on.

But what I knew — perhaps "perceived" better describes it — was vague. All-over-the-place. Disparate, unorganized bits-and-pieces that gradually started coming together for me as I began my television-writing career. Because, to my great good fortune, *I was the freelancer being helped along, coached, by the seasoned writer/producers and story editors for whom I was writing scripts.*

In truth, I was being *paid* to *learn* from these practical-minded, experienced *professional* storytellers — writers who, *selfishly*, wanted *me* to succeed in order to make *their* lives easier. To hold my hand so that, when I turned in my final draft, they wouldn't have to rewrite me from page one.

Not everyone is so lucky.

In this book you will be struck — often, I hope — by flashes of "whoa, of *course*" recognition. Stuff about writing which till now you've "sort of" understood, that will suddenly become distinct for you, viewable from a fresh perspective. *Learnable* techniques for creating solid, well-made, page-turning, audience-holding stories, whether fiction or fact, from thrillers to cozies, romance or memoir.

Self-editing tools you'll file away in your mental checklist.

Once learned they should help free you from a lot of those nagging mysteries about writing, the sometimes daunting *mechanics* of the process that can so easily get in the way of inspiration — of art — and of the *delicious* pleasure that can be had from writing well.

Put another way that should be clear to anyone who has tried writing, the *creative* side — the side that is *art* — is difficult enough without the added burden of insufficient knowledge about the form – an understanding of fundamental storytelling techniques. Again, *that* is what this book is about.

I would like to assure you that what it is definitely *not* about is formula — about rules (though I *will* cite a few suggestions that come close) — about academic terminology such as *secondary theme*. Nor is it about the necessity as some will tell you that this or that transition or story-move *must* take place at a specific point. *That* I leave to those authorities who, though they may have never earned twenty-eight cents as fiction writers, seem to have it all figured out.

In a very real way, this book is about troubleshooting your own writing. To illustrate, below are a series of phrases heard repeatedly in TV story and script meetings:

> "What're the bad guys doing? We need to
> keep them alive."

"Where's the heat? This is a non-scene. It needs an edge."

"Maybe give the guy a condition – hay-fever, a cold, an allergy, why don't you? Or he's cranky, tired. Or indigestion maybe. Or he isn't getting enough sex."

"The scene on pages twenty-five through twenty-seven is talky. Tighten it up."

"Lose the girlfriend, or give her an arc. Right now, she doesn't take us anywhere."

"His one-eighty comes out of left-field. Platform it back in Act One."

Working as a writer/producer in network series television, these are the kinds of story-problems – and solutions – one has *got* to learn to identify.

All of which has a *very* direct application to *each* of us, what-ever we write – romantic comedy, suspense, science fiction, horror, mystery, satire, juvenile, historical and on and on. Because we *all* need to recognize and *remedy* those same problems – and others – in our *own* output. Call it self-editing, or distancing, or objectivity – it all comes to the same thing(s). In part, to avoid falling hopelessly in love with what we've written. To regard nothing we've done – until we're finally ready to part with it, to give birth to it – as etched in stone. It's about learning to *see and then fix* those problems I quoted above – and a lot more that you'll hopefully learn to pick up on while reading this book.

Sure, some of you may luck out, as I did, and be taught on-the-job by professionals. But that doesn't happen often. The truth is, *none* of us can *count* on finding an editor who will zero in on those problems in our manuscripts, point them out to us – and offer solutions. That is something else this book is about. Simply put – the techniques you'll discover here will help to equip *you* to know *what* you're writing – and *why* you're writing it.

Again, nothing you'll learn from these pages is a substitute for Art. But they contain some answers, some tools, that should liberate you creatively, since presumably you'll be fighting fewer doubts and questions about the Craft.

Writing – even when we know these things – is for most of us rarely easy. That said, it is my sincere hope this book will help you to *enjoy* the process – to take increased *pleasure* from your writing.

Because *that* is what it's all about.

Tom Sawyer
Malibu, California
www.ThomasBSawyer.com

ONE

THE WRITER'S MINDSET

Before moving into the mechanics and techniques I learned in the TV business, I want to pass along several points that I consider essential to success as a writer, no matter your medium or genre. Together, they form a kind of fundamental, philosophical grounding, a foundation. The place we should *all* be coming from.

I am certain that I could not have succeeded in that field — or any other — without acquiring this type of pragmatic mindset and, I submit, neither will you achieve your full potential until you do so.

Face it — We're *Entertainers*

First, and perhaps most important, the writer must understand that *no matter what it is* we're trying to communicate — to readers or viewers — be it comedy, drama, instructional or informational, high art or lowbrow — we want our audience to *respond* — to laugh, cry, *feel*. We want to surprise and delight and yes, when possible, teach and illuminate. And to achieve that, to get our message across, we *must entertain*.

We *are* entertainers.

Now, that is not as tacky/shallow as it may sound. We — all of us, no matter how lofty our literary intentions — want an audience, or we *hope* to find one, for what we have to say — and we want to hold its attention. Strike that: we *must* hold its attention — or we won't get our story across. To accomplish that, we *must* — in some way, tasteful or not — entertain. It's an obligation. This is true whether we're poets, peddlers or preachers.

Or even trial lawyers. The noted novelist/attorney Scott Turow has said that when he was first hired as a prosecutor he was astonished to find that "the trial lawyer's job and the novelist's were...shockingly similar. The trial lawyer who lost the audience also inevitably lost the case. Engaging the jury was indispensable...Tell them a good story..."

The TV Writer's Mandate

Ancillary to the concept that we are entertainers, and arguably just as important, is the mandate in commercial television that — while it's unique to the medium — should resonate for all of us: In simple, *the television scriptwriter's mission is to deliver the audience to the commercial break.*

That's the job. That's *all* of it.

It is the advertisers who are paying the bills.

And how does the TV writer do that? By keeping the audience *entertained.* Fascinated. Curious. Amused. Moved.

The TV writer is not *obligated* to elevate the public's cultural level, to educate, inspire, enlighten, or to produce art. But neither are we *prohibited* from doing so (with the obvious exception of shows that are so abysmally dumb in conception as to make such aspirations impossible — there have always been too many of those, but I prefer to celebrate the remarkable few that are brilliant — and yet manage to survive in this mass medium). If the writer aims for any or all of these last, that's great, but it is *not* a requirement.

The *only* requirement is that the audience *must* continue to watch. Hence, if the television writer fails to grab, and then hang onto viewers, if the audience switches channels *before* the commercial — *if the writer loses the audience,* that writer is not doing his or her job.

Is not the same thing true of the poet, playwright, novelist, biographer – or clergy? Several years ago I delivered a seminar at a

Baptist writers' conference. About 20% of the several hundred attending the talk were ministers. They were there to learn how to hold their congregants' attention.

The TV Writer's Bogeyman

Another take on it: an imperative that television taught me, is that as I write each word, each line of dialogue, I keep a certain image in mind — that of a representative, metaphorical VIEWER. Mine happens to be a guy in his tee-shirt, feet up on the coffee table, sitting there after another long, tiring day at a job he despises, a beer in one hand and the remote in his other. And *that's* the important part — the *remote* — because his thumb is constantly hovering over the channel-selector button. He is ready to vote, moment-to-moment, on how well I am doing *my* job. If I bore this guy, for even an instant, I've lost him. Ergo, I have failed.

Oh — and there's another side to this guy — as I envision him — that sets him apart from, say, the moviegoer in a theater. The moviegoer has *paid* to see the film and, beyond his cash investment, is at least somewhat captive; he's sitting in a dark room, which contributes to his feeling of isolation and therefore to his concentration on the movie, which is bombarding his senses with Surround-Sound, special effects and a giant screen. The person reading your novel or short story is, you hope, likewise *engrossed*. My TV viewer, on the other hand, is seated in a lighted room, looking at a small screen while the kids are screaming, the dishwasher is clattering, the phone is ringing and the dog is farting. *And* if that weren't bad enough, every few minutes he's further distracted from *my* show by — commercials.

Think about it.

That's the challenge.

How different is it from the necessity, in writing a novel, that you grip your reader? Or the movie that rivets the audience's attention, advertising copy that sells, or essays, newspaper stories, travel articles, or even memoirs that compel us to read on? Or weaving a story that sways a jury? How different is it from the historian's obligation to hold the attention of the reader who bought his or her book? Or the playwright's to the audience that paid for tickets to the show — to keep the people in — or better yet, *on* — the edge of their seats — instead of walking out?

The novelist whose reader stops turning the pages is not doing his or her job.

The advertising copywriter whose words don't rivet the customer – and sell the product – isn't doing her job.

The minister whose flock dozes off or begins fidgeting, glancing around the room, isn't getting his message across. A successful pastor whom I know approaches his sermons with the following philosophy: "I try to comfort the disturbed, and disturb the comfortable."

We *want* our audiences to be absorbed, *hooked*. We want them to stay with us, turn the pages, remain in the theater. So we *must* remember — *always* — even in the smallest, seemingly least important scene — that we *cannot bore them*. If we do, they'll stop reading or watching or paying attention to whatever it is we're trying to say. And even the most dedicated — the ones who despite the boredom hang on till the end, will find the process torturous. And will therefore be reluctant to try anything else that we've authored.

That is the standard by which *you* must judge the words *you* write. *And* you've got to be willing to revise them or dump them if they don't measure up — *no matter how deeply you might admire them.*

The Hitchcock Motto

Perhaps the most meaningful words for a writer that I have ever encountered came from a filmmaker. Alfred Hitchcock, the master writer/director of suspense movies said:

"Drama is real life — with the dull parts left out."

I think about that a lot. And so should you. It applies to all of us, to *all* kinds of fiction writing. *You*, the *writer*, the *teller* of your story, have to *locate*, to *recognize* — and then present — the heat. The *drama*.

And by "drama," I mean comedy as well as tragedy, and all of the shadings in between — including surprises — *all* of which have, at their core, a common and arguably the *single* most important thread for writer and audience — *CONFLICT.*

But more to the point, and I'll expand upon this later, *show* the *conflict. Play* it. Don't talk about it, or have your characters discuss it. *Dramatize* it. *Focus* on it. Set up scenes or situations that *use* it, that *illustrate* it. *Conceive* your stories *and* your characters *and* your individual scenes and moments *in terms of conflict*. In terms of *disagreement. Argument.*

Conflict is a word you will find repeated *many* times in this book — for very good reasons.

Because conflict *is* the story.

Moreover, the above – along with so much else in this book – is not limited to fiction writing. The Hitchcock Motto is particularly relevant for those who are telling a "true" story — be it history, biography or a memoir. That a story is factual gives it, admittedly, a measure of cachet, but *only* a degree. Its success depends on how *well* it is told.

A true story consisting of a succession of this-happened-and-then-that-happened-accounts of how your hero and/or heroine met this-or-that famous person, or was present when some noteworthy event took place — that doesn't cut it. Where was the *heat* in their tale? Where was the *theater*? What were their *emotions*? Where was the *excitement*?

Because, nonfiction or fiction, you must still *entertain* your audience. Put another way, readers/viewers *want* to see, to experience vicariously, the *obstacles* your protagonists overcome in getting from A-to-B-to-C. Not *just* that they get there. I believe that historians or biographers who have a dramatist's sensibilities, a gift for going beyond the academic, write the best, most satisfying, riveting *non*fiction. People with the fiction writer's talent for finding the *real, human* meanings, the stuff that takes us *past* the dryness of dates and times and places, enabling us to *identify* with the players.

The Computer in Your Head

As most of us know, among the wonderful features of writing on a computer are such functions as the spell-checker, grammar checker, the thesaurus, and the search-and-global-change capabilities. They have made the act of writing a very different process than it was in the days of Dostoevsky, of Shakespeare, or even those of Fitzgerald. In fact, when I read something as complicated as Dostoevsky's *Crime and Punishment* and think about his having written it in longhand, I am not merely awed — the thought gives me a headache.

Part of what I hope you'll acquire from this book is a set of computer-like *mental* functions to augment those that come with your word-processing software. A mental checklist (though there's nothing that says you can't write this stuff down) of criteria that you'll punch up in your head, which will help you to see into your manuscript and alert you — in the same way your computer reminds you of misspellings or questionable grammar — to some of the no-no's of fiction writing. A set of standards — of tests to which you subject your literary output.

It's called *Self*-editing.

Certainly, in the best of all worlds, you'll hire an editor, or your publisher will assign one. Or you'll be lucky, as I have been, and writers more knowledgeable than yourself will hold *your* hand — for a while, anyway.

But...

Do not *expect* anyone else to tell you exactly what's wrong with your work. Don't count on it. Why? Because at the very *best*, even their *informed* comments will be to some extent subjective.

And at the other end of that equation — to quote the immortal words of the great screenwriter/novelist, William Goldman — **"Nobody knows *anything*."**

In between there may be gradations — a teacher or mentor, an agent or editor who knows more than you do, who may make constructive suggestions.

But ultimately, *you* must be the judge of what you write. And you must *believe* in it, and in *yourself*, because I guarantee, there will be (in case you haven't *already* discovered this) a *lot* of people who — either intentionally or well-meaning — will say and do things that will discourage you.

What I'm talking about is that if you hope to become an effective writer, you *must* develop your *own* highly tuned self-editor — forgive the bluntness — your own *shit-detector.*

It is my hope that a lot of what you'll find in this book will become *part* of you as a writer, part of your standards, of your *craft*. And your art. The word-processor in your head.

Write to The Money

Still another dictum that travels well from TV writing to other forms, "*Write to The Money*" is *not* a plea on behalf of commercial hackdom. What it *is* is a reminder that we *must* remember whom and/or what our story is about. One of the tenets in series television is that the star of the show should be present in *at least* every other scene. Why? Because presumably your star is the reason the audience tunes in to watch the show. In other forms of fiction writing it means that your protagonist, the star of *your* piece, is the one the reader wants to follow. It means that, while you may wish to insert other threads in your story, you must guard against losing your major character's arc.

You have *got* to keep your lead character *alive* — and *moving* the action.

First, it's about fixing in your mind just *whom* the star of your show is, your lead character (or characters). *That* is the one your story should focus upon, the one your audience *cares* about, wants to *know* about. But more significantly, *that* character should be *driving* your story. *Making* it happen.

Essentially, the *star* of your show (or play or novel or short story) – your *protagonist – should be the engine of his (or her) <u>own</u> salvation* (or destruction, if that's what your story is about).

The same should be true of *any* character you want your audience to root for.

One of the most frequent errors committed by inexperienced writers is that of allowing the heroine or hero's problems to be solved by someone else. Or worse than that, by happenstance, as in having a key clue fall, with no effort, into the detective hero's lap, instead of — say — using his or her wits to find it, or, arguably better, to trick the killer into confessing.

Likewise, *victims* do not usually make interesting, compelling protagonists. Frank McCourt, in his brilliant autobiographical *Angela's Ashes*, may have been a victim at the outset, may have even felt like one, but he rose above it, extricated himself from his situation, driving his own story.

Okay — so, as stated above, what we're talking about here is getting ourselves into a no-nonsense mode about what we do. A place we feel comfortable about.

We entertain people, right?

Not rocket science.

TWO

BEGINNINGS — THE STORY IDEA

Asking Yourself "Where's The Heat?"

There is a single word that embodies the place where the writer's head should be at *all* times.

The place from which you start – and finish.

It is a word you've already seen – and will see again – repeated in this book – one *you* should repeat like a mantra, till it's *engraved* in your brain: Conflict.

Conflict. Conflict. Conflict. Conflict.

Throughout this book you'll find words like "edge," "heat," "difficulty," "problem," etc., all of them variations on "conflict."

Without conflict *there is no story*.

Without conflict within a scene, you have a *non-scene*.

Drama, or comedy, is about *characters in conflict* with each other, with their situations or their environment.

In children's literature, the latter two are almost a given. And for those of you who write science-fiction, the list of conflict-sources includes androids, mutants, renegade computers, hostile planets, force-fields and other challenges not-yet-invented.

All of these conflicts are — or should be — roadblocks that interfere with your characters' efforts to get from A to B, preventing them from attaining their *goals*.

The point — the validity — the *necessity* — of adopting this mindset about conflict, of keeping it *automatically at the front of your mind*, from the conception of your story, all the way to the end, will become more apparent as you read this book.

A Word or Two About Originality

During my career in TV, where one has to generate a *lot* of stories, the question I've been asked most frequently by far is — *where do you get your ideas?*

Well, I *steal* them. And it's a technique I highly recommend.

But with a few caveats. Steal the *good* stuff. Don't steal junk. Steal from the classics, from *Hamlet* to *Casablanca*. From *Romeo and Juliet* to *The Maltese Falcon* to *The Phantom of the Opera* and *Frankenstein*.

In case the foregoing tempts you to stop reading any further, I ask that you hang in there for the next few sentences, because you are about to learn one of the most valuable lessons a fiction writer can know. Which is:

> **Anybody** **who believes they're going come up with a fresh, original plot, a story that's never been told before, leads a far-too-rich fantasy life.**
>
> **There are *no* new stories.**
>
> **There are *no* new plots.**
>
> **They were *all* used up *before* Shakespeare ever started. They were all used up in the Bible and, almost certainly, long before that, by folks dressed in hairy-mammoth skins, sitting around bonfires, beating the earth with clubs as they embroidered their accounts of hunting expeditions or battles with rival tribespersons.**

> **In fact, William Shakespeare maintained that there were only nine basic plots (or six or eleven, depending upon which account one chooses to believe). In the 1800's a Frenchman, Georges Polti, defined thirty-six of them, some of which, it can be argued, are simply modifications of others.**
> **No one, as far as I know, claims there are more.**

As writers, what we *do* with stories is *recycle* them. Knowingly or unknowingly.

Knowingly is better.

Basically, they're all of them sort of folk tales *to which we apply our own particular spin.*

That's what makes them special. *That's* how we make them *ours.*

Each of us views the world through our own personal, one-of-a-kind filters. That's the essence of art, of what *any* artist does.

A brief note about how I have, over the years, borrowed or stolen outright from Dashiell Hammett's classic, seminal modern detective story, *The Maltese Falcon*, may serve to illustrate my point:

I was a kid when I first read the novel, and therefore didn't really understand it's significant place in American literature. It took me several readings – of it *and* the competition – to absorb the many ways that it differed from virtually all the mystery and detective fiction that had gone before – dramatically breaking the patterns set by Arthur Conan Doyle (*Sherlock Holmes*) and Agatha Christie (*Miss Marple & Hercule Poirot*, among others). It also became apparent that most of the mystery fiction written since has been largely imitative of *The Maltese Falcon*, with *very* very little even close to equaling it. Of course there has been, and continues to be, some terrific writing done in the genre, but for me, while Raymond Chandler's wonderful, literate *Philip Marlowe* novels came nearest, *Falcon* has never been surpassed.

One of the ways Hammett's paradigm novel was so singular was that while it contained a murder mystery – Who killed Sam Spade's partner, Miles Archer? – it was, surprisingly for its time, a detective story that was *not* about *clues*. Another difference was that the tale took the reader on such a fascinating, entertaining journey through rascal-and-double-cross country that one almost forgot the murder mystery part of it. In the end, Hammett delivered satisfying closure in the matter of Archer's killer, but in truth we almost didn't care, the rest of it being so thoroughly gripping, introducing us to such a variety of wonderful, skewed characters – especially his enigmatic hero, private eye Sam Spade, and the lying, seductive Brigid O'Shaughnessy, who was to become the model female antagonist of novels and films noir for decades. The superb, classic movie version of *The Maltese Falcon* (Scr. & Dir. John Huston) is, by the way, almost scene-for-scene and word-for-word, Hammett's book.

When I began writing for the *Murder, She Wrote* TV series (Cr. William Link & Richard Levinson and Peter Fischer), before it went on the air, Peter Fischer explained to me that he envisioned the show in the mold of traditional Agatha Christie puzzle mysteries (most of which predated Hammett). I pointed out to Peter that as a boy I had read a few Christies, plus a couple of locked-room mysteries by others, and they had bored the hell out of me. I added that I wouldn't write that sort of thing for him. Peter asked what I *would* write. I said I'd write *The Maltese Falcon*. Peter's reply was "That'll be fine."

For the next twelve years, that's mostly what I wrote and/or generated and oversaw. And except for a few connoisseurs, I doubt that many viewers were aware that *Falcon* was my prototype.

Your model, your favorite, that book or group of books that has touched you, may be "literary," or trashy, obscure or best-seller, pulp fiction, Thomas Mann or Shakespeare. What matters is that you try to understand the material itself, and why you respond to it. As a writer, it is well worth *your* time to analyze it, and to study what the author did to make his or her words speak to you.

Okay, so you've based *your* story on some tale that resonates for you. Sometimes the source will be instantly recognizable to the audience. Sometimes not. The ancient Greek legend of *Pygmalion*, has variously been retold in children's' literature as both *Sleeping Beauty* and *Cinderella*, was written in more modern terms as a stageplay (also called *Pygmalion*) by George Bernard Shaw, and filmed in 1938 (Scr. Shaw, W.P. Lipscomb, Cecil Lewis, Ian Dalrymple & Anthony Asquith – Dir. Asquith & Leslie Howard). Which in turn spawned *My Fair Lady* (Scr. Alan Jay Lerner, based on the musical play by Lerner & Frederick Loewe – Dir. George Cukor). The tale was filmed more recently as *Pretty Woman* (Scr. J.F. Lawton – Dir. Garry Marshall). Not to mention numerous more obscure variants.

Occasionally we encounter stories that *seem* original.

They're not, though there are a few created in modern times that come close. Franz Kafka's brilliant short story, *Metamorphosis*, is one of them. It has meaning on several levels, including difference and prejudice and magic. Yet reduced to its core essentials, it is a story about — as the title indicates — change.

But when a story is told more freshly than others, when it *feels* as if we haven't been there, it is a tribute to the author. And when that happens some audiences love it — and for others it can be *too* fresh — or unfamiliar. Consider the work of such writers as Thomas Pynchon, Donald Barthelme or Samuel Beckett. The enemies of their more extreme, off-the-wall output are almost as vocal as their advocates. A movie example: *Being John Malkovich* (Scr. Charlie Kaufman – Dir. Spike Jonze) was for me the most original film I had seen in many years. A lot of people hated it for the many of the same reasons that I loved it — it was for them *too* inventive. One of my biggest reasons for loving it, incidentally, was that I could *not* have written it. When John Cusack emerged from the elevator onto the 12-and-1/2th floor, they had me. I knew that I was in the presence of original minds. For me, *almost* up there with Mel Brooks' overhead shot of the chorus in the devastatingly funny *Springtime for Hitler* production number in his landmark comedy, *The Producers* (Scr. & Dir. Mel Brooks). Likewise, *The Truman Show* (Scr. Andrew Niccol – Dir. Peter Weir) and *Sliding Doors* (Scr. & Dir. Peter Howitt) felt fresh

— as if I hadn't seen them before. And yet, *all* of them have their roots in oft-told tales.

Feeling fresh.

That shouldn't be a lot to ask, but it is.

While on the subject of originality, I'd like to impart a suggestion for avoiding clichés in your prose as well as in your story-telling. A technique I've tried to impose on my own writing – a kind of discipline, really – another aspect of the Writer's Mindset: Train yourself to recognize when you're employing common, often-heard or hackneyed phrases – and – if it isn't intentional (as, for instance, a character who's *supposed* to speak in clichés), either eliminate it, or rephrase the cliché so that it takes on a fresh(er) flavor. In a way, this can be viewed as reinventing – or tweaking – the familiar.

A simple example: instead of using the one about someone's "ears burning" (presumably because another has been talking about that person), why not vary it with "heating up," "sizzling," "simmering" or the like? While the foregoing are hardly brilliant, they give the phrase a slightly more thought-out feel – as if it wasn't just tossed-off, the first thing that popped into the writer's head (*not* a good advertisement for one's writing). And when used in dialogue, a fresh turn of cliché makes a similar statement about the character who speaks the lines.

Stealing Stories From Oneself

If writers always obeyed the old "write about what you know" slogan, there would be no Science Fiction, Stephen King, fairy tales, nor Shakespeare, to name a few. Unless "what you know" includes human behavior and mental processes.

It goes virtually without saying that often the most fruitful source of story material is one's *own* life — the things we've *experienced*, the *people* we've known. The *characters*, both good and bad, with whom we've shared the stage. All of them provide potential story material. For instance, a number of years ago I had a fascinating — and simultaneously horrifying — encounter (a business association, actually) with an individual who, it gradually became apparent, was a pathological liar — a person who literally could not tell the truth about *any*thing. Anyone reading this who has been closely involved with such an individual will recognize that which I'm describing. He became the basis for an unusual antagonist in one of my TV scripts. That, along with some other types of psychopathology is dealt with in greater detail in Chapter Four.

On a more prosaic level, during my writing career I've created characters and entire stories by pirating the foibles and virtues of friends, famous people, my mother, father, in-laws, two wives and my own – and others' – children, as well as myself. If you are not already doing so, you should.

Predictability

While it is generally *not* a good idea to tell stories in such a way that your audience is "ahead" of you, sensing how this or that thread is going to turn out, there are exceptions. Predictability *can* be useful, as in, say, telling a story like the *Titanic* disaster, with its epic inevitability. But *only* if the journey on which you take your audience toward that known ending is full of surprises — is not of itself predictable.

Another way to make predictability work *for* you is a technique familiar to writers and readers of mysteries: misdirection. Take your audience down a path that *seems* obvious, and then surprise them by swerving at the last moment onto another route. In writing any kind of puzzle-mystery, it's good to be aware that you're playing a game with your readers or viewers, that unless they're very young children, they're probably hip to the rhythms of such stories, and are trying to outguess you. Which is why in TV, I tried to avoid what I call the *Perry Mason* (Wr. Erle Stanley Gardner) set-up wherein you introduce a half-dozen characters, one of whom is absolutely beastly to everyone else in the show, thus giving all of them motives — and then you'd kill him. What kind of surprise is that? The viewers *expect* him to die because he's a mean sonofabitch — *and because they've seen it before*.

Worse, if that's what you deliver, you'll lose your audience. So, one of my favorite gags was to choose, as the murder victim, a character so minor that he or she had had only one or two lines of dialogue. Or none. A victim for whom there *were* no obvious murder motives. Another alternate was to make the victim an *unintended* target — a character in the wrong place at the wrong moment.

Essentially, all this means is – think surprise. Think about what you've set your audience up to expect — and then flop the coin – or give the rug a good yank. They'll love you for it.

The Story *Idea*

Let's start with a question: what does a good story consist of? I'm sure you have read and/or heard about all sorts of theory and/or rules, from *the three-act structure* to *Aristotelian concepts* to *fugeddabout-the-three-act-structure-it's-old-hat* to *this-has-to-happen-before-that-can-happen* to who-knows-what. From *you must start with a theme* to the necessity of summing up your theme in a few well-chosen words (such as *a story about seeking-and-not-finding*) to not even *thinking* about the "meaning" of what you're writing.

Incidentally, with regard to starting with theme, I find that it often tends to force the writer to plug in archetypal, symbolic, not altogether human characters. A couple of notable examples are John Steinbeck's *East of Eden*, and Herman Melville's *Billy Budd*. Both are allegories about good (or innocence) versus evil, both undeniably powerful, but for me the effect was diluted by the black-and-whiteness of the characters.

Nonetheless, some of the theories are arguably valid.

Some of them.

But before dealing with those points, there are three *even more* basic elements of storytelling — a set of criteria — an acid test — again, a *mindset* – that have worked very effectively for me in my writing career. Fundamentals that enable us – long before we get into the details, the complexities of our stories, the poetry of our writing, our narrative voice, point-of-view and so forth – to examine whether or not we're *starting* it right. Three key essentials, without *any* one of which — to put it bluntly — *your story ain't gonna work.* I call them The Three C's (forgive the somewhat cutesy-poo alliteration — but it makes them easier to remember):

Conflict

Characters

Construction

Now, you're probably muttering to yourself that these are *obvious* requirements for a well-written story.

And you're right. Yet over time I have been astonished on more occasions than I can recall by *professional* writers — people who should know better — who have overlooked one or more of them. Most frequently the first — Conflict.

So — back to the initial question: what constitutes a *good* story idea, and what comprises good storytelling?

For now, let's deal with the first part. The idea. The nugget. Your premise. The *essence* of a good, workable story. Where does it come from? What does it start with? In the following section on *Pitching*, several approaches are covered – including the *what-if*, the *key-scene*, and the *Old Movie Shorthand.* And in a very real way, these examples also embody aspects of *how* to *find* your story, to discover – sometimes to your own surprise – *what* it's *really* about, and *communicate* it succinctly and *effectively.* To others – and just as importantly – to yourself. Again, first off, it *must* at least suggest, or imply, the central *conflict.* And if it suggests one or more secondary conflicts, that's not necessarily bad.

A story idea: Two long-feuding entertainers are forced to face each other – and themselves – when their grown children fall in love.

Obviously, a take on Shakespeare's *Romeo and Juliet* – but instead of the tragic ending, we add the following: the young lovers' relationship is strained almost to the breaking point when it looks as if one of the parents has attempted to kill the other.

Not a monumental premise, *but* workable – *and* the main conflicts are clear.

Pitching

In television and film, pitching is the way stories are sold. Again, while you may never find yourself in a similar situation, the techniques of successful pitching have a *lot* of relevance, and *great* importance, for *any*one who writes, from poets to novelists to ad-copy writers.

Because pitching is very much about being clear and un-fuzzy in your own head about what it is that you want to write.

Pitching your story well means that, over and above whatever gifts you may have as a salesperson, YOU understand – and can express to YOURSELF – what it is you're going to write!

In television, as in much of life, pitching, selling (AKA: the dog-and-pony show) – is a con job.

A confidence game.

Not, however, in a (necessarily) pejorative sense, but rather in the *literal* definition of the term. The object of the game is to instill in the person to whom the writer is pitching, the *confidence* that the writer can deliver the goods, can accomplish what he or she claims to be capable of – in this case, delivering a good script.

In television, we mostly "pitch" stories for series episodes, or pilots or for movies, verbally, in one or two sentences. We often refer to these pitches as "TV Guide Loglines." That's right. Those concise show-descriptions you've been reading for years in *TV Guide* are the way we sell them to the producer, the star, the studio-or-network executive or whoever it is who can say yes or no. Such pitches are also referred to as "hooks," or "springboards." They contain the *essence* of the story.

A good pitch is concise, articulate, and *entertaining*. In more cold-blooded terms, a good pitch is one that *sells*. One that gets the writer an assignment.

The good pitch also says something important about the writer

– about how he or she will *approach* the story. *How* it will be told. How solid a grasp the writer has of what it's *really* about.

But perhaps the single most important element of a good pitch is that it either suggests (if you're trying for subtlety) or (better yet), *spells out* the main *conflict*. In the publishing business, it's that quotable bullet that sets apart the idea for a novel, the one that succinctly *says* what it's about, that can make it a "big" book.

A story premise or situation that compels you – or your listener(s) –to involuntarily begin imagining the reactions of an established character, or characters, can be highly effective, both in selling the idea, *and* clarifying it for yourself.

From there, if the *pitchees* are sufficiently hooked, the writer gives them a brief, verbal beginning-middle-end breakdown. In the case of a pitch for a series pilot, a movie or miniseries, the writer usually provides a *"leave-behind,"* a written proposal of from two to ten-or-so pages.

Here are a few examples of verbal pitches:

Murder, She Wrote premise. "A vampire comes to Cabot Cove."

That was the pitch, in its entirety. Two young women with almost no credits gave me that line, and we were in business. The expanded pitch was that a mysterious man, who *appears* to be a vampire, buys an old Victorian house. He was, incidentally, *not* the murderer-of-the-week — nor was he the murder victim. And although the conflict isn't described in so many words, it *is* implicit; in that single sentence we immediately *see* the possibilities — the arguments between those townspeople who believe it's a "real" vampire and those who do not — the reverberations, fears and angst that will arise, the *drama* it can create. And especially of course, we visualize the reaction of our practical-minded heroine, Jessica Fletcher who, we know, will say, "Wait a minute...a *vampire*...?"

Again, a *Murder, She Wrote* pitch. "Let's do *Pagliacci* and *Casablanca* in Cabot Cove" (in TV, the shorthand of pitching variations on movies, stageplays, etc., is fairly common currency; they're within almost everyone's frame of reference). The *Pagliacci* (Libretto

& Music, Ruggero Leoncavallo) part: a small three-person carnival comes to town. The carny-owner, his boorish second-banana, and the boor's long-suffering, attractive 40ish wife. The *Casablanca* (Scr. Julius J. Epstein, Philip G. Epstein and Howard Koch, from the play, *Everybody Goes to Rick's,* by Murray Burnett and Joan Alison – Dir. Michael Curtiz) part: the attractive wife goes to the Sheriff's office to obtain permits. The Sheriff turns, and finds himself face-to-face with the woman who dumped him 20 years ago in college and ran off with their classmate, the boor.

Parenthetically, you may have noticed that though *Murder* is part of the show's title, in neither of the above *Murder, She Wrote* pitches was there mention of the murders themselves. There's a reason: murder was a *given.* Further, *Murder, She Wrote*'s murders were rather sanitized, almost never the result of psychopathology, as in the real world of, say, serial killers or Columbine High School or the like. And, they were never grisly. We avoided decapitation, mutilation or death-by-torture. Therefore, the motives were pretty much limited to money, sex or power (or occasionally, the wrong person getting killed), which we likewise tried to vary from episode to episode. Similarly, we were largely unconcerned – especially at the pitch-stage – with how the murder or murders were committed. The method simply had to be different from the ones employed in the last four or five shows — so we wouldn't appear to be repeating ourselves.

Another TV series episode pitch, for *Supertrain,* a rip-off of *The Love Boat* (Cr. W.L. Baumes – Inspired by Jeraldine Saunders' book, *The Love Boats*), but taking place instead on a futuristic railroad train. *Supertrain,* incidentally, was so monumentally awful that where it's listed in reference sources, the writers appear to have removed their names, leaving only then-network-head Fred Silverman to take the rap for its creation (a rather delicious irony, since it was allegedly his brain-child).

My pitch was that we do *Journey Into Fear* (Eric Ambler) and *Lost Horizon* (James Hilton). That hooked 'em. The story: A revolutionary new, secret anti-aging cream is being transported from one coast to the other. Immensely valuable, it is sought by the Bad Guys, who want to steal it and make Big Bucks. And they're willing to kill for it. Our protagonist has it, and is their target (that's the *Journey Into Fear* part). Also on the train is a beautiful young (apparently) woman. By the time the train reaches New York, while the protagonist has managed to outwit and vanquish the Bad Guys, the effects of the seemingly miraculous cream have worn off, and the woman, living proof that the cream works, looks her age (she's really in her nineties – the *Lost Horizon* part). That was the pitch in its entirety. *Supertrain,* incidentally, was mercifully killed before I could write the script (at that fledgling point in my career, I sought almost any work I could get).

And another. For *Kaz* (Cr. Don Carlos Dunaway & Ron Liebman), I was asked to write an episode – it was pitched to me, the freelancer, by the head-writer, Sam Rolfe, after he'd rejected my own story suggestions – in which the protagonist/trial lawyer (played by Ron Liebman) defends a battered wife who has murdered her husband. That was all they gave me.

Over the next few days I researched the subject of wife-beaters, and those women who had been imprisoned for killing them, and became infuriated at the injustice of it all. I told the show-runners that I would *only* write the script if the murder was dead-bang premeditated, and the wife is acquitted. I wanted the show to serve as a message to wife-beaters that their wives could kill them and get away with it. That was *my* pitch.

Rolfe and company agreed, with the wise proviso that we not inform the network that that was our purpose. Had CBS known we intended to suggest that murder is sometimes justifiable, they would have undoubtedly forbidden it. The reason: because of commercial sponsors' abject fear of consumer backlash, and the networks' dread of offending advertisers, the unspoken rule was – and still is – that shows can only pretend to be *about* something – that if a statement is made about a controversial subject, it *must* be balanced by showing the other side of the argument. This is particularly true of "moral" questions. And, if the issue is too "hot-button," they won't go near it in the first place.

I constructed my script so that the murder was committed while the husband was asleep in a chair (he hadn't beaten her for several days) – and our lawyer-hero wins the battered-wife an acquittal by arguing self-defense – from the inevitable next beating, the next and the next.

The satisfaction I got from writing that episode, and seeing it produced, was exponentially increased when it aired, and generated thousands of letters applauding the point we had made. Women's rights groups requested copies of the script.

As you can see from these examples of pitches, they jump-start your imagination. *You* begin to write the rest of the story, *seeing* pieces of it in your mind. *Visualizing the conflicts*. In television, that's what is *supposed* to happen with the people to whom the story is pitched. *They* begin to fill in the blanks.

A successful pitch is one that *excites*, that
starts your *listener* mentally writing the
rest of your story.

For writers of *any* kind of fiction, it's a good way to *think*. Because by pitching your story – to a friend, spouse, publisher, editor – but *particularly* to yourself – *you* will gain a better, firmer handle on it. *You* will be less likely to marry yourself to an incomplete premise, or to a story that goes nowhere. *Most* important, it's about *clarity*. About *knowing* what your story is about – and then maintaining your focus.

As stated, the above pitches did not have beginnings, middles or ends. They were not full-blown *stories*. That's a good way to start.

But *only* to start.

Unfortunately, too many inexperienced writers dive straight off these springboards into the actual writing of scenes, of script or narrative. And days, weeks, or months later, discouraged, they place their partially finished manuscripts in a desk-drawer, because they were unable to figure out where their story should go. This problem will be addressed shortly, including ways to avoid it.

Envisioning a specific incident or moment or scene are good ways to *start* generating a story. As described earlier, a what-if-this-or-that-were-to-happen? Or a scene that, for instance, illustrates a premise. Again, an example. I was producing a series called *The Law & Harry McGraw* (Cr. Peter Fischer), which co-starred the remarkable Jerry Orbach as an old-fashioned, seedy, Philip Marlowe/Sam Spade-type Private Detective whose Boston office was across the corridor from patrician Attorney Eleanor McGinnis, portrayed with sexy elegance by Barbara Babcock. And I thought it would be interesting to play a climactic, turning-point scene in which Harry is not merely baffled by the case he's pursuing — but he's reached the point where he is *abjectly defeated*, ready to throw in the towel, to quit the detective game — and Ellie tries mightily to talk him out of it. And seemingly fails, but while she's doing so, Harry figures out the mystery.

That was the scene I wanted to write — mostly because I could almost *see* the electricity, the *fun* Jerry and Barbara could have with it. And more importantly, the fun I, and my archetypal Viewer would have watching it.

But I had no story. Only questions. How could I get my characters *to* that place? And even trickier, could I pull it off so that it wouldn't feel contrived?

The story I constructed in order to get to that scene pitted Harry, with his plodding, gumshoe methods, his beat-up car, etc., against a slick young hotshot PI who was into computers, Ferrari's, electronics and so forth — all of the latest techniques. Both detectives would work on the same case, with the increasingly discouraged Harry always several humiliating steps behind the new guy — except that in the end, Harry wins out; he solves the case the old-fashioned way — with his instincts and his gift for bullshitting people.

That key scene around which I built the story — the *moment* I was going for — took place deep in the third act (out of four TV acts). In theatrical terms it would have been the opening scene of Act Three, wherein I begin to bring my protagonist out of the tree, when the by-then profoundly discouraged Harry has hit bottom, convinced he's a has-been, a dinosaur who's past it. He's given up on the case, on himself, and then, abruptly, it all turns. Harry suddenly sees it clearly — *how* the crime was committed, and *what he must do* to smoke out the bad guy. The script, and that scene, are among my favorites.

The above-cited example could also be described as kicking off a story with a character, because in that instance, Harry McGraw's attributes and hang-ups were a known quantity, as were Ellie McGinnis's. I wanted to put them into a situation which would dramatize who, at bottom, they were, bringing their individual chemistries to bear on each other.

You might very well begin thinking about *your* story with a situation that is *not* as pivotal as the foregoing example. I've done so, many times. In any case, it's another workable approach to developing a story idea.

Again, however, *only* a beginning. But arriving at your premise via a specific scene, and then reducing it to its core idea is a good exercise, a habit worth developing to keep you on top of the story you're telling, to keep it from getting away from you — a reminder *for you* of where it's *supposed* to be going.

A novel is something else. As is a full-length movie. The longer forms are not always so readily summed up in one or two lines. When they can be, it's often because there isn't enough *story*. And yet, even if you're writing a complex novel, you *should* be able to describe it in fewer than 100 words. Not synopsize it (that should come to two or three pages double-spaced) — but *essence* it.

Okay, so a hook — or a bare-bones premise — isn't a story, any more than are those one or two scenes you've envisioned for your novel or screenplay — scenes you can see so vividly you can almost taste them — moments you can barely wait to commit to paper — or kilobytes. Yes, there *are* writers who can sit down and type CHAPTER ONE, or FADE IN, without a clear idea of where they're going, without an image of a complete story, without really *knowing* their characters, and, through the sheer weight of their talents, one hundred-twenty — or four hundred pages later — they will have written a successful screenplay or novel.

I am not one of them, though you *may* be.

But – particularly if you're a beginner, I wouldn't bet on it, and neither should you.

Sorry guys, but the next step is — for most of us — the *hard* part. The **s-t-o-r-y**. With a beginning, middle and end. In TV it is *demanded* of most writers because the producers need to be confident that they – and the writer – know *where* the story is going, to make sure it's consistent with their series, and to ensure that they're not buying a script that's too similar to one they've already shot.

Oh – and in case you ever *happen* find yourself in a face-to-face pitching situation – wear something blue. For reasons that probably aren't worth analyzing, your words will be more convincing, more believable, if you wear some blue.

THREE

The Process

Building Your Story

Yes, this is where I invoke the often-dreaded "O" word.

Outline

I continue to be amazed by the number of working, published novelists I meet who do *not* outline. And at the risk (one from which I have rarely shied) of coming off as a smartass – *they are wrong*.

I hasten to point out that they are not necessarily *bad* writers. Some great writers work that way (on a tightrope, without a net). What I *am* suggesting – and this is both arguable and unprovable – is that their work – their end-product – would probably be even better if they had outlined.

My next argument, however, is almost inarguable: writing a long, complex piece such as a novel or screenplay from an outline *will* make the entire process easier, less angst-ridden, and – except for those of you with masochistic tendencies, far more pleasurable and satisfying. And, as with the Great Ones, your finished story will be better.

Okay, here's how it's done in television, and how *you* should do it.

From that initial pitch or premise, we expand our story to a page or two. A manageable size that enables us to *grasp* the whole, to embrace the *totality* of it at a glance so that you can, among other things, question its roundness, its shape. So that, as mentioned earlier, instead of getting mired in details too early in the game, we can *see*, at all times in the process, *where* we are going. To maintain *control* over our material, instead of the other way around — instead of, as is so often the case with inexperienced writers, having it overwhelm us. Overcoming or guarding against that danger is, in essence, what this process is all about.

From that expanded-but-still-brief narrative description of our story, we go to what is referred to as a *step outline*. Most one-hour TV episodes are divided into a "tease," and then four acts, a form governed largely by the necessity for commercial breaks. In the average one-hour episode (actually, about 44 minutes of story), there are between 30 and 40 or more scenes. The step outline consists of two-to-four line narrative descriptions of what happens in each scene, which in a few pages, again permits us to maintain our grasp on the shape of the entire show. And, if a line or two of dialogue helps nail a scene, there is no law against using it in lieu of, or with narrative.

Some writers, incidentally, prefer to jot their scene descriptions on file cards that they can arrange on the floor, or tack to a bulletin board, reshuffling them in this or that order to better tell the story. There is at least one software program designed for that purpose. Whatever the method, it's about maintaining that all-important overview.

One of the ways we start breaking down the show into steps is to divide a legal pad page into quarters – one for each act. That way, we can easily envision how we'll build to the moment just preceding each commercial break, or "Act-Out." Also described by TV writers as the "oh, shit," it's that instant when the story is interrupted, the players left in a situation suspenseful (or funny or dramatic) enough to keep the audience glued through the sales pitches – in order to find out what happens next (not a bad way to end the chapters of a novel).

Because not only must we keep them watching *till* the break, we have to make sure they'll still be there *afterwards*, so they'll stay tuned till the *next* batch of advertisements. Laying out your story – and writing it *to* your Act-Outs is covered additionally in Chapter Five, *Construction – Telling Your Story*.

It's worth noting that in television, at this point the writer usually "talks" the steps to the writer/producer(s) — and often, to story editors — who offer comments, fixes, recommendations for improving the structure. This might include telling the writer that this "beat" (scene) or that story-move is too similar to one they're already employing in another episode. These observations are as a rule accompanied by a back-and-forth discussion, including helpful, *problem-solving* suggestions on the order of "Okay, suppose we do it this way..." These script or story conferences are usually audiotaped (and the tape is then given to the writer if he hasn't brought his own cassette recorder). One major benefit of taping is that, rather than needing to focus on taking notes, the writer can take an active part in the discussion. The additional obvious plus is that the writer comes away from the meeting with a complete set of notes.

I mention all this because, while most of you will never write a TV script on assignment, nor even wish to do so, you may be a member of a writing group, or have contemplated joining one — and tape recording the comments that are thrown out during such a session can be invaluable in revising your work, or reminding you of thoughts you had during the meeting. The same would apply to any lengthy verbal commentary about your writing. When I teach writing courses or speak at seminars, I urge the attendees to tape the sessions. As with the TV scriptwriter, it facilitates *participation*, rather than trying to be a stenographer.

Incidentally, during the development of a TV script there's a somewhat sneaky business-reason these initial "steps" are presented verbally, rather than in writing. According to the Writers Guild of America contract, we (the buyers) are entitled (from the writer) to two drafts of the story and two drafts (plus a polish) of the teleplay. That's what we agree to pay for. Were we to ask for any additional drafts, we'd have to pay extra — hence the writer is almost never asked for more. If we were to accept, on paper, the step outline, we would by Guild rules have to count it as the first draft of the story. Everyone involved understands that this is, technically, a way around the WGA contract, but I have yet to encounter a writer who objected to the procedure. It helps everyone concerned. And there are times when the writer, after presenting the outline in "step" form, skips the next phase; with some action-adventure shows on which I've worked, the step outline *is* the story outline — that's as far as it's taken — and the writer then goes directly to teleplay. Definitely *not* the case with more complex dramatic pieces, for which the scene-by-scene narrative outlines (albeit sometimes including scraps of dialogue) run from 20 to as many as 35 double-spaced pages (which is longer than average for TV), leading to a 55 page final script.

For those of you who write in other forms, the meaning of all this is to *emphasize* that no matter *how* eager you are to get into the meat of the story you wish to tell — *write an outline first*. Lay it out. More about that later, but first, in case you're not clear:

What is a Story Outline and How Does it Differ From a Synopsis or a Treatment?

A synopsis is generally defined as a one-to-four page narrative description of what happens in your story, *told with some sizzle*, since it will likely be used as a selling tool – to entice an agent, publisher, or producer to take a look at your manuscript.

A film treatment *used* to consist of twenty-to-forty or more pages of narrative. That seems to have changed. In Hollywood, where it is rumored that few people will (or *can*) read, and even fewer have attention spans longer than five minutes, treatments have become so brief that the line between them and synopses is blurred. I have had producers caution me that *anything* longer than four pages is death. Even for the purposes of selling the screen rights to a novel.

An outline is a different animal. As mentioned above, it's a scene-by-scene breakdown (continuity) of your story, written (basically) in narrative form. The length and amount of detail can vary, and style need not be a concern unless you plan to show it to others who might not "get" it. For TV and film scripts that are written on assignment (rather than on spec), the outline will invariably be read by producers and often by non-writers, such as studio or network executives, and should therefore be written with such exposure in mind. But if your outline is for your eyes only, the writing can be sketchier.

Because of my background in TV and my own comfort-level, spec or not, I still write my outlines in some detail. The outline for my novel, *The Sixteenth Man*, was 112 pages. Thus, for me, the outline for each scene of a TV script might run half a page to a page, double (or 1.5) spaced.

What Does a Story Outline Look Like?

Outlining can be rather daunting and, for those unfamiliar with the process, it may be difficult to imagine the form – not that there *is* a single, rigid style. To acquire a self-created example I suggest that you try a technique I've found both enlightening about the form and instructional about writing — a method by which you can learn how good stories (and those not-so-good) are constructed. Even experienced writers, including professionals, may find it to be a few well-spent hours.

Rent or buy or borrow a videotape or DVD or other type of recording of one of your favorite movies or shows or miniseries (or one that is *not* a favorite, but was nonetheless an artistic or commercial success). View the first scene, punch *Pause*, and write three or four or five lines about what the scene was about. Then run the second scene, and repeat the process — and so on and so on. It will take awhile, but by the time you're through, you will have an outline. You'll *see* what it looks like, *know* how it's supposed to read.

But more than that, you will have *learned*. A lot. You'll *see* what the writer was *doing* — *understand* it on a fresh level. Which can be a revelation.

One *More* Plea (But *Not* the Last)
On Behalf of Outlining
        or
How the "Drudgery" of Writing Your Outline
***Will* Turn Into Pleasure**

While the high-wire act of writing a novel, play or screenplay without knowing your characters or where they – or your story – are going *may* be exhilarating, it can — and often does — result in the *unfinished-manuscript-in-the-desk-drawer syndrome*, with its accompanying discouragement and depression.

I don't know about you, but I am not into that type of risk of my time and efforts, nor do I recommend it for others.

Working from an outline will make you a better writer in a hurry.

Yes, I've heard the argument that – having outlined – the actual writing process then becomes one of "filling in the blanks." *And* the one about how the author sacrifices spontaneity. Or the potential for inspiration.

Nonsense.

Did the great painters not work from sketches? Does anyone suppose Beethoven composed his *Ninth Symphony* without having a pretty solid idea of where he was going?

As mentioned, building your story in this way will give you *control* over your writing. You'll *see* the things that are working, and the things that aren't. The unities — and the disunities. The flow. The repetitions. It is a lot easier to fix a story at the outline stage than it is after you've written — and sweated — 80,000 words, and find that on some intrinsic level it doesn't work. Or that you don't need that chapter, or this character. Or that you've gone off in a direction that works against your narrative.

Or, worst-case, once you start making changes — the entire structure begins to collapse.

In TV we call that kind of after-the-fact phenomenon "pulling threads." A most-disheartening experience for a writer.

By outlining, you can avoid such disasters. Your outline is where you construct — and more easily deconstruct and/or reconstruct — your story.

Whether you work with file cards on a bulletin-board, or a computer program, or scribble on a legal pad, your outline will, for instance, enable you to *look critically* at each scene, each situation, to judge how it fits into the whole of your story — the *dynamic*. You'll see how you've *paced* your story. Where it sags, where it needs help. You'll make *discoveries* about your characters. It will help you maintain balance — and that *so* necessary objectivity, or "distance." If there isn't enough edge or angst or heat inherent in a scene or a setup or a chapter, you'll have a far better chance of recognizing it, being able to *fix* it, adding to your mix. If consecutive scenes are too much alike — or too jarringly different, you'll see it. Is this scene too long, that one too short? Is there enough incident – *stuff* happening — or too much? Are you maintaining your desired focus? Is there a hole in your plot? Is your story entertaining enough, *compelling* enough?

I'm convinced that with few exceptions, whatever reasons a writer gives for working without the net provided by an outline, what it *really* means is "I'm too lazy to work the kinks out of my story ahead of time."

Can successful novels, plays and movies be written that way? Sure. It's your call. But *know* this:

Outlining *will* help you and your writing – and it *can* save you from disaster. Viewing it another way – do you want to win – or lose? Are you willing to gamble your time on another uncompleted project? I'm not. In my own writing, assuming my story idea survives the outline stage, I finish what I start.

Conflict Defined

It's important to understand that conflict is not necessarily warfare, or yelling and screaming. In fact, the conflicts within your story *should* be of varied intensity, orchestrated by you so that they are not all the same. It's how the great composers write their music – how you should write yours.

There are writers who may disagree with my insistence that there be *some level of conflict* in *every* scene. In fact, there have been a few I've worked with in television who questioned it. But unless those writers came around to my approach, that was the end of our work-relationship. I suggest that you adopt a similar tenet for your own efforts.

A shipwreck victim *easily* reaching a nearby reef is dull. The child getting to the cookie jar *without difficulty* is uninteresting. Why? *Because the goals are too-effortlessly achieved. Show* your reader the swimmer overcoming hazards — from an inability to swim, to high seas and pounding surf, to sharks or... *Dramatize* the child straining to reach the cookies, in danger of falling off the shaky chair on which she's standing. On the verge of being caught, and perhaps breaking the family heirloom cookie jar. Or give it a non-physical edge, the child's emotional struggle, feeling guilty or wary because she's been warned against it. All are variations of conflict. Problems that add *texture* (sometimes referred to as *color*) to the story you're telling. Even problems so tiny that they're sometimes not immediately or obviously identifiable as conflict.

Can you have too much conflict? Sure.

Is it possible that the problems you place in your characters' paths might be repetitive — too similar? Sure. Conflicts that follow a recognizable, *predictable* pattern. In TV we describe that as writing "by-the-numbers."

What about levels of intensity — can there be too much heat? Absolutely. We've all read books or seen action movies where the explosions, the special effects crashes-and-clashes are so frequent and so big that they anesthetize us.

Incident-after-incident at the same high emotional pitch tends to work against itself, dulling all of it. Similarly, the audience can become just as stupefied by too many slow scenes in a row. You should aim for an up-and-down dynamic — not only from scene-to-scene, but also moment-to-moment *within* your scenes. More about that later. That's part of self-editing your work. It's another way you'll benefit from writing your outline.

About Texture

An excellent example of texture is embodied in a memorable scene in the brilliant 1954 movie classic, *On the Waterfront*. Remarkable for its screenplay by Budd Schulberg (suggested by a series of articles written by Malcom Johnson), and it's direction by Elia Kazan, the film also features a number of dazzling acting performances, all of them overshadowed by that of the young Marlon Brando who, in this and other roles of that era literally reinvented the art of acting.

In *Waterfront*, Brando portrays a likeable, unschooled, slightly punch-drunk, failed prizefighter/dock worker. His co-star, played by Eva Marie Saint, is a shy, sheltered, convent-schooled young woman. Early in their relationship there is a wonderfully con-structed walking-talking scene, tentative, guarded, full of subtextual tension. She's somewhat afraid of him, of his strength. He's intimi-dated by her gentility, her education. As they stroll along the Hoboken waterfront, conversing uneasily, Ms. Saint drops one of her knitted gloves. Brando picks it up, but to her minor surprise and con-fusion, he doesn't give it back to her. Instead, as their verbal sparring continues, he uses it to gain control. Still talking, he sits on a child's swing and idly pulls the small glove onto his large hand. She watches, running her lines (neither speaking of the glove, nor reach-ing for it) and *we* watch and listen — *fascinated* by this little piece of business into which all sorts of subtext can be read. We sense that she's distracted by what he's doing, that she must fight to stay on-subject. And he seems to recognize the advantage, using it to play with her. It is a marvelous moment in a marvelous, landmark scene. Ironically, it was *not* scripted, but rather invented — adlibbed — on the spot when Ms. Saint *accidentally* dropped her glove. Brando retrieved it, continued the scene without missing a beat. So our sense that she was distracted is accurate. Like the audience, she was riveted by what he was doing. That Kazan had the inspired judgment to let the camera run is a tribute to his brilliance. Students of film history know it as *"The Glove Scene,"* and while the way it turned out wasn't *written on the page*, it was in effect written by the actors and the director. And more to the point, it stands as a model, the kind of moment we, as writers, should stretch ourselves to reach.

That's theater. That's entertainment. That's good, edgy writing — but *mainly* — it's a form of *conflict* — the place *from* which *you* should consciously approach *your* writing — until it becomes so much a part of you that you no longer need to think about it. Till you *automatically* ask yourself *"Where's the heat?"*

An exercise: Next time you write a scene in which your characters are, say, in a kitchen, have one of them making a pot of coffee while the other character's (or characters') dialogue is playing out. Then – consider adding a problem that seems unrelated to the conversation — the Mr. Coffee malfunctions, he or she can't find the scoop that is usually left in the coffee can. A distraction, which now becomes part of the scene, possibly making it necessary for the other person to assist, or become irritated by having to repeat a statement. From there it's easy to see how much more lively your writing can become. In theater/film parlance it's called *business*, and as in the Brando example, actors often come up with it on their own. And sometimes directors create it. But since I *cannot* count on either of the above, I *write* it into my scripts (as well as into my prose). I urge you to do the same, no matter what form *your* storytelling takes. Listen carefully, for example, to the next professional joke-teller you see; if the gag is longer than a one-liner, most likely he or she will have loaded the buildup with *business* that adds to the humor, stuff that has you laughing long before the punchline. Flavor. Texture. Entertainment.

Red Flags

Perhaps the *most* valuable gift you give yourself by writing your outline is getting stuck.

That's right. Reaching that point where the forward thrust of your story screeches to a halt. We've all experienced it – you just plain *cannot* figure out where your story should go next — that desperate "I know, maybe if I have my characters do X" moment when you begin *forcing* the next scene, and the next, hoping they'll inspire you — until you realize you're writing *fill*.

In my experience as a TV writer, the above-described Flag (*fill*) usually means one thing.

Not enough story. Not enough *complication*.

Not enough going on – problems, goals, angst, urgency or whatever – to sustain audience-interest – or your characters' – or yours – for the full 44 minutes — or whatever length your story happens to be. Such a Flag almost always signals a need for another layer of complexity. Sometimes adding a minor subplot takes care of it. Sometimes an additional character or two. Or you need to make your adversary smarter.

Okay, once again it's write-it-on-your-forehead-time: **When you have <u>enough</u> story, the question of what should take place next almost *never* arises – and if it does, it's usually easily answered.**

Another Flag that is, happily, likely to make itself known during the outline process is the discovery that one of your characters is serving no purpose, save for possibly one or two small points. If reading this rings no bells for you, I guarantee that it will the next time you encounter it in your writing. And when you notice that you've got such an extraneous, not-really-necessary character, the usual solution is to dump him-or-her-or-it, or to combine that character with another.

The purely "mechanical" scene or moment is another place to beware, another flag that will often show up in your outline. What do I mean? In TV we describe as "mechanical" those points in a story that have must be portrayed in order to clarify and/or advance the plot, yet serve *no* other purpose. Incidents or actions which may be so perfunctory that the inexperienced writer, just to get 'em in there, will write them in an uninteresting manner.

Example: For whatever reason your story demands that you show your protagonist purchasing – say – a train ticket. If you are unable to make the transaction part of a larger, more interesting scene, if it must stand alone, find a way to make it work in terms of conflict that will, ideally, test and expose your major character, the scene's protagonist. How do you pull it off? Let me suggest one or two.

The ticket clerk has an attitude or eccentricity that your protagonist finds irritating – or comical. Or, the clerk is impatient, or distracted, having – say – just lost a contact lens (the important point is that it *generates* a reaction – an *edge*).

Or – another traveler, late for his or her train, rudely tries to elbow past your protagonist who, maybe out of sympathy, defers to the harried customer. And perhaps the ticket clerk takes a particular point-of-view, figures the protagonist is being too tolerant.

Conflict = entertainment.

And in the process, we can learn something new about our protagonist.

Another symptom of *fill* is the scene or chapter in which the story stands still – the place at which, despite all the dialogue or character-stuff or action you've just written, leaves your players in substantially the same place they were at the beginning. Not good. Again, the important point here is learning to *recognize* the Flag. Often, the fix will require nothing more than moving them a bit closer to their overall goals, or throwing the next obstacle across the path of one or more characters.

These are a few of the Red Flags we *all* encounter as writers. The trick is learning to quickly, instinctively recognize them — *and* what they're telling us. And how much better to detect them — and fix the glitches — in the outline-stage — *before* you are faced with tearing apart your carefully-written work. The aforementioned *Pulling Threads.*

Put another way, there are few tasks more depressing than having to *fundamentally* rewrite a work to which we've devoted months, or worse, years.

Some writers however are *into* pain.

If you're one of them – *get over it*.

Big Flags, little Flags. A carefully constructed outline isn't a cure-all for rewriting, nor will it guarantee that you'll put together a story that makes sense.

But it *can't* hurt.

Oh, yeah – I've heard the often-used argument that outlining hampers creativity. Not true.

Play the Moments — Don't Just Talk About Them

In film and television that phrase is near the top of the writer's checklist. *Play* your characters' big emotional moments, their turning points, their battles, their deaths, their wins and their losses. *Dramatize* them. *Write* them. Make *scenes* out of them.

That seems so obvious, yet over and over I have been amazed to see, in the work of otherwise gifted writers, even some very successful professionals, the biggest scenes taking place off-screen, stage or page. Or, *if* they're played, often blunted. I have a hunch it is less about ineptitude than it is the natural inclination of most of us to shy away from highly emotional moments in our personal lives, especially our over-civilized desire to avoid confrontation. Or *real* thoughts of death and/or violence.

I first encountered this phenomenon in a script-meeting early in my TV career. I was one of three or four staffers who were giving notes to a freelance writer before sending him off to do a final draft of his teleplay, which was about a young mentally retarded man – and the question of his ability to live on his own after his father/guardian's sudden death. The writer had come up with a quiet scene at the gravesite, wherein the grieving, mentally challenged young man spoke to his late father.

The discussion among the writers was about *what* the young man should say. A suggestion pushed by the scriptwriter was to have him quietly sing the theme song from the character's favorite TV show, *Gilligan's Island* (Cr. Sherwood Schwartz – Comp. Schwartz & George Wyle). Other notions included some maudlin, on-the-nose remarks about how he missed the old man. Happily, these were quickly rejected.

Then I offered that it might be appropriate, and moving, and startlingly *real*, to have him express his anger at dad for having died, for deserting him. Such resentment and animosity are very human, almost universal reactions to the death of a loved one. What *surprised* me were the reactions from my fellow writers. It was more than just flat, academic rejection. Several actually *resented* the idea – angered that I'd brought it up. *All* of them looked at me as if I'd suggested that the young retarded man unzip his fly and expose himself on-camera. I quickly shut up – realizing that clearly, I had inadvertently crossed into some off-limits territory.

We settled for a shot of him squatting by his father's grave, rocking back-and-forth on his heels, singing the *Gilligan's Island* song (a lovely performance by Adam Arkin). Emotionally, it was about a 4. It was – okay.

I believe, incidentally, that this resistance to having our deeper emotions touched is one of the reasons so much of America's theater, cinema and television are such uninvolving, surface, escapist enter-tainments. This becomes especially clear when we compare our slick, big-budget movies with the better films from, say, France or Italy or Sweden. They are *different* from American movies, and the difference goes far beyond language. For me the most significant disparity is in point-of-view – a kind of *basic approach*. European films tend to be *closely observed*, highly personal and emotionally charged on levels rarely seen in American product, wherein the deepest emotional demands on the audience seem mostly to be made by explosions, car crashes or gunplay. Think of *Cinema Paradiso* (Scr. & Dir. Giuseppe Tornatore), *Il Postino* (Scr. Giacomo & Furio Scarpelli, Massimo Troisi, Anna Pavignano, Michael Radford – Dir. Michael Radford), or the films of Claude Lelouch, Federico Fellini or Ingmar Bergman.

An illustration: In *Cinema Paradiso* there is a scene of parting. People embracing, saying, or expressing their goodbyes with their eyes, their faces. And there is a shot of an aged, gnarled, blue-veined hand on the shoulder of another. The camera lingers on that hand, and the moment is deeply touching.

For me, that shot *essences* the difference between European films and those made in the U.S. With few exceptions (Spielberg comes to mind) I cannot *imagine* an American blockbuster-director even framing such a picture, much less including it in the final cut.

Yes, there are a few American films as emotionally affecting, equally intimate. An example is contained in a scene from one of the *truly* great Westerns, *The Outlaw Josie Wales* (Scr. Philip Kaufman and Sonia Chernus, based on the novel *Gone to Texas*, by Forrest Carter – Dir. Clint Eastwood). In it there is the gut-wrenching moment when Josie (portrayed by Clint Eastwood) realizes that his family has been slain. The audience suffers his pain, and I'm sure many who watched it were brought to tears, as I was. Compare that to a similar story-point in a far more typical, white-bread-and-mayonnaise, emotionally uninvolving American movie, *Gladiator* (Scr. David Franzoni, John Logan, William Nicholson – Story: David Franzoni – Dir. Ridley Scott). Early in that big, technically impressive film, the protagonist, a Roman General played by Russell Crowe, returns to his bucolic, rural home after a lengthy, exhausting battle-campaign – and discovers his wife and son murdered. This moment *should* have been powerful, deeply moving, tearing the audience to pieces as does the one in *Josie Wales*. Instead, it is curiously, almost *startlingly* distant. The audience sits there watching – feeling almost no connection with the character *or* the tragedy. A *little* sad for him, maybe, but definitely not pit-of-the-stomach, or even lump-in-the-throat.

Was it because of Crowe's performance? Choice of camera placement or angle? Or the way it was lit? Or might it have been *fear* on the part of the artists involved (chiefly, the director and producers) to confront their own emotions. I suspect it was all of those and more.

I believe it's part of an overall mindfix which seems to govern American entertainments in general. That Hollywood and Broadway perceive American audiences as being largely uninterested – if not outright resistant to – heavy emotional content may even be an accurate reading, though I question its validity. Nonetheless, that perception explains to *my* satisfaction why so many of the works created by our entertainment industry seem to be conceived *and* presented at *arm's-length* from the audience.

Part of the equation is, I suppose, economics. Small movies with large emotional content rarely become blockbusters – which in our system means that not many are produced. And when they are, they receive only limited distribution. Another factor may be in the American Psyche itself – insofar as it is understood by the creators of our entertainments – a desire to escape, to avoid for a few hours having to think or feel, or to deal with reality. Which may to some extent account for much of modern art's popularity – a preference for emotionally undemanding wall-decoration rather than the substance and often-visceral pull of, say, a painting by John Singer Sargent or Edgar Degas.

In musical theater, the history of this phenomenon extends at least as far back as Britain's Gilbert and Sullivan, Viennese Operettas, and no doubt beyond. But on Broadway, the "Musical" (an odd noun, when one thinks about it – a musical *what?*) has elevated shallowness, banality and cleverness to an almost-religious cult status. Yes, many of them contain admirable, well-written popular tunes, clever lyrics and book, superb production, sterling performances, inventive choreography, great costume-and-set-design and often-amazing stagecraft.

And an emotional bite that's right up there with mayonnaise.

We sit there tapping our toes, admiring the show cerebrally, sort of – or even largely – enjoying the experience, yet not really *connecting*. Too often, for myself anyway, an hour later I can barely recall the show. Did I have a pleasant evening? Sure. But at those prices I expect more than pleasant. I've often wondered what it's an escape *to?*

Admittedly we're talking about forms that are intended to *simply* entertain – certainly a worthwhile goal. Oftentimes toe-tapping, laughing and humming the songs (or the scenery) on your way home *is* enough. And who knows, maybe the Hollywood/Broadway folks have it right. Perhaps there *does* exist a kind of ingrained national opposition to having our deeper emotions assaulted or manipulated – as if in a way it's a violation of our privacy.

Nonetheless, while it's undoubtedly true that few of us *want* a steady diet of profundity or intense feeling, my *own* boredom with much of what I read and/or view, my *own* sense of having wasted my time, tells me there's a market for *far* more thought-and-emotion-provoking, more deeply involving material than the small amount we're given.

The point is that in *any* case, denying or avoiding emotion is emphatically *not* what being an artist *should* be about.

It is not what good writing is about.

If *you* are interested in moving your audience, connecting with your readers on below-surface levels, I suggest that you study, and borrow or steal, from the European filmmakers and Italian opera. Yes, there's always the risk of descending into mawk and melodrama — but I'm convinced that it is better to err in that direction – and then if you must, dial it back – than to *aim* for blandness.

Don't be afraid to <u>use</u> the power your words can have.

Remember that guy with the remote in his hand.

Back to the notion of *playing* the moments, another way of stating it, another worthwhile axiom from the visual media:

Don't *tell* us about it — *show* it!

And still another TV *Don't*: Avoid having your characters, or your narrator, talk about yet-to-appear off-stage characters, players the audience has never met. As in, "When I worked for Dave Mason…" or "Margaret is going to the show tonight…" when we've not *met* Margaret or Dave Mason (unless they're about to come onstage – or it's intentional foreshadowing). Why? Because it's confusing, and until the viewer – or your reader – can put a face to the character, largely meaningless.

Of course there will be, and have been, significant and totally valid exceptions, such as in Eugene O'Neill's *The Iceman Cometh*, where the entrance of Hickey is much anticipated. Or Clifford Odets' *Waiting for Lefty*. And certainly, Samuel Beckett's *Waiting for Godot* (who never does show up – or does he?), and others that employ such references to foreshadow the arrival of someone new – and important. In mysteries it's a common device. But generally, a lot of talk about characters who haven't appeared, or worse, aren't going to appear, is a flag to be wary about.

Another term from television (and movies) that you should know and understand, because it will help you identify what's important in the story you're telling is:

The Money Scene

The facedown on the dusty Western street, the big emotional moment between two of your characters, the climactic battle, or the solitary protagonist's instant of revelation. In film and television the term usually – but not always – connotes the big, expensive-to-shoot moment(s) in the show. Sometimes it's the scene with dozens or even hundreds of extras. Sometimes it's the party scene, or the big car chase or special-effects-and-stunt-laden action blowoff. In Musical Theater they're referred to as Production Numbers. Grand Opera usually has at least one per show.

A story or script or novel can have several of them.

For the director of a television dramatic series, who has to shoot eight-to-ten pages of script per day in order to finish on schedule, the term can take on a meaning particularly relevant to the writer of narrative fiction. The director, in breaking down the script ("prepping" and/or scheduling the shoot), may see that of two comparable three-page scenes, one seems less important than the other in terms

of theatrical or story value (more commonly, in TV the writer/
producer will point it out). So the director will allot, say, thirty minutes to shoot the less-crucial scene, and perhaps several hours to shoot
the other.

How is this accomplished? Often by minimizing the choreography within the less vital scene, by reducing number of camera
setups or moves, each of which can eat up time relighting the set or
location. Shooting the scene in a single "take," with no cuts, also
speeds things up. The more expensive money scene will then be
filmed with greater care, devoting extra attention to sophisticated
camerawork and/or lighting, more "production value," thus heightening its significance for the audience.

Okay, that's how it works on the screen. But what we're talking about here really isn't significantly different for writers of
narrative prose. It's about deciding how much relative weight to give
to the various parts of your story. Some just don't *need* three or four
pages. Others will require more. Sometimes it's only a matter of short-
handing the less important stuff.

Which at bottom is about knowing what *doesn't* need to be
emphasized in your story. Which steps or moments or transactions are
not worth dramatizing or showing – usually because they're obvious
and/or without sufficient entertainment value to justify their inclu-
sion. This subject is addressed in some detail in Chapter Five. For
now, however, let's deal with identifying and amplifying the material
that *counts* – your money scenes.

Often, money scenes are not big production scenes, but rather
are turning-points – moments in the story where events suddenly go
in unexpected directions. A scene for example in which the writer
might have to make an extra effort to *justify* such a turn for the audience. In *The Sixteenth Man*, one of the most crucial and challenging
money scenes occurred when my protagonist, Charlie Callan, was
faced with a complex series of truly epic *personal* choices, all of them
trumped finally by a *moral* decision of historic importance for which
there was no "right" answer: *what* should he do with the hard evidence

in his possession *of who really killed President John F. Kennedy?*

It was a largely internal struggle in which the path Charlie finally chose could easily have been regarded by my audience as stupid or unbelievable – thus causing readers to lose sympathy for him, or worse, to very probably stop reading the book.

I knew that, *given the limitations of who he was*, I *must* show Charlie considering as many shadings of risk-versus-gain as he was capable of handling – this flawed, very human guy whom I hoped my readers would find as fascinating as I did. He had to weigh his over-all situation, the effect his decision might have on his loved ones – while all along factoring in his emotions, his finances, and *his* sense of the realities. And – Charlie would finish up the whole process with a choice that, while farfetched, arguably crazy, and almost certain to end badly – *had* to seem to him (this character I had created, who was *speaking to me*), the *only* course he could have chosen.

But even more importantly, for the readers it had to be *inevitable* – they *had* to *believe* it and to go *with* Charlie, to root for him. To say *yeah, crazy as it seems, if I were Charlie, I'd probably have done the same thing*. This also falls under the heading of "bolstering" (justifying) your story-moves.

The key point here, for the writer of fictional comedy or drama, as well as history, biography or memoir, is that you must learn to identify your own money scenes, and then give them appropriate weight.

The Plot Device

Appropriately named, Plot Devices are story-tools that can help us tell ours more effectively, with more pop, zip, emotion, motivation, or whatever we need a little more of. The following are gags that have been employed – and often abused – in endless variations for as long as people have been telling stories. The trick, as always, is to employ a fresh spin, to avoid having it come across as cliché. Not always easy. Some, such as the conveniently unlocked door, present more of a challenge than others.

Plot Devices: Clocks

Clocks are *extremely* useful energizing devices. A clock is nothing more than a deadline – a time-limit. As in: Something *bad* will happen unless the money (or whatever) is delivered by such and such a time. Or, the mortgage has to be paid up by one o'clock tomorrow afternoon or else they're going to foreclose. Or, if the ransom isn't paid at a certain hour, the kidnap victim is going to be killed. Time-bombs. *Literally* ticking clocks.

It's tried, true, often hackneyed, but it *works*.

In TV we refer to some generic clocks via dialogue, as in the bad guy-line: "Okay, then we're moving up the shipment. It'll hafta go out now, instead of at ten o'clock." Shorthanded as *"The Old Moving-Up-The-Shipment Gag,"* it usually means that the undercover hero, who has arranged a police-raid for ten o'clock and, unable to alert the cops to the revised schedule, will have no choice but to try saving the day on his own – at great personal risk, of course. Sound familiar? While your clock must sometimes be disguised in order to avoid being flagged as a cliché, it can nonetheless add needed urgency and/or suspense to your story, and angst for your characters, neither of which has a downside.

Plot Devices: Maguffins

The maguffin is the object of great value that almost everybody in the story is after. Sometimes it's the secret plans. Sometimes it's the computer disk, or the microchip. In Dashiell Hammett's *The Maltese Falcon,* the maguffin is the Falcon itself, a legendary jewel-encrusted golden statuette. Sometimes it's the most valuable diamond in the world. Or the suitcase full of money that your protagonist has mistakenly picked up from the airport luggage carousel.

Occasionally the maguffin is a desirable woman, especially in Film Noir, wherein the traditional setup consists of two men who want the same extremely sexy female. Badly enough to kill for her. For the gag to work, of course, she is usually untrustworthy, and *always* to die for. For me, the ultimate, definitive film noir is *Out of the Past* (Scr.

James M. Cain, Frank Fenton, and Geoffrey Homes, from Homes' novel, *Build My Gallows High* – Dir. Jacques Tourneur). And it didn't hurt that the leading man was the perfect noir hero, Robert Mitchum, nor that his co-star, Jane Greer, was the ideal, sultry Object of Desire.

A bit of advice in choosing a maguffin: nothing becomes dated more quickly the latest high-tech item.

Plot Devices: Hiding in Plain Sight

The photograph or video that inadvertently records something (an event, a person, object, or other image or information) that should not have been seen by the camera. Or the clue that was always there for everyone to see, but it's so obvious that for awhile it's ignored.

The potted houseplant, its shoots pointed away from the adjacent window because it was rotated when someone removed the door key concealed beneath it.

The map or document that consists of more than is apparent at first glance. Or, the crucial information is invisible to the naked eye, only discernable in, say, UV light. A map containing hidden data was used to wonderful effect in one of the truly classic, still eminently watchable WWII movies, *Five Graves to Cairo* (Scr. Charles Brackett, Billy Wilder, based on Lajos Biro's play, *Hotel Imperial* – Dir. Billy Wilder).

Plot Devices: Meet-Cute

For decades, the meet-cute (sometimes referred to as "cute-meet") device has been virtually a required ingredient of Hollywood's Romantic Comedies. To the point of wearing out its welcome because it became so obvious, so often. And yet it endures because, when well-executed, it can very effectively set the tone for one's story. It's that first-meeting, boy-girl scene (now of course it may be boy-boy or girl-girl) where he accidentally spills his tray of food on her expensive gown, or she is demonstrating her tennis forehand and inadvertently knocks him in the head, or he or she falls into the swimming pool. Usually, in the older films, and in today's as well, the result for the remainder of the first two Acts is that while he's wild about her, she can't stand him (the "wrong-guy-who's-really-Mister Right" gag) – or, vice-versa, he resents her, but she has the hots for him. Or, neither likes the other until fate, or the plotting of friends, brings them together again and shows them the Light.

There have been many, many takes on the meet-cute gag, some of them tedious, many of them wildly inventive and/or laudable. But for me none surpasses its use in the unforgettable *And Now, My Love* (Scr. Claude Lelouch, Pierre Uytterhoeven – Dir. Claude Lelouch). In this timeless movie, the meeting of the two lovers – and it *is* cute – doesn't take place until the *final minute* of the film. And delicious it is – though if you've never seen the movie, I caution you to try viewing in its almost-impossible-to-find original French (with titles), since the dubbed version is a horror, truly an atrocity committed against this work of art.

While the meet-cute has arguably been overused, it *works*. But the writer who becomes familiar with some of the many variations has a far better chance of coming up with an inventive approach.

Plot Devices: Platforming

Arguably a technique as much as it is a device, platforming, as used in TV, is in many ways another term for foreshadowing. Particularly when it's about laying in the hint of an event-to-come, a twist, a clue, or character-nuance-or-change. It's about planting something physical, verbal or descriptive at one or more points in your story, that will pay-off later. Or, so that when a certain event occurs, it won't seem too jarringly out-of-character-or-place, or provide the wrong kind of surprise — the kind that can cause one's audience to quit, or walk away disappointed. Or worse, angry.

But you need not necessarily worry about platforming when you're writing or outlining page one. Often it is accomplished deep into the work, when the writer realizes the need to "set-up" an action by going back to earlier scenes and plugging in related references or incidents.

Again, in *The Sixteenth Man,* the fact that protagonist Charlie Callan was a former minor-league pitcher whose arm had gone dead played a key part in the narrative, *and* in the central mystery. But until I was nearing the end of my outline I didn't realize just how important it was; it necessitated my going back through the story and inserting (platforming) moments that emphasized his passion for baseball, his experiences as a player.

In mystery writing, starting – in your head – with the solution, and then working backward is a common approach. In my case, concocting TV mysteries, once we had the premise, the central "play" that was the heart of each show, we almost invariably worked backward from the "Gotcha" scene. This meant laying in the clues, the evidence, including the all-important *"Play-Fair Clue"* (more on that later), the murderer's slip-ups if any, and the detective's observations that eventually led to the real killer. In my own scripts, however, I seldom decided who the murderer was until I had almost finished the outline. At that point I had a better fix on who might be shaping up as the least likely assassin. Occasionally for me – in the mystery writer's ongoing game of trying to outwit the audience – figuring my viewers had already zeroed in on that ploy, I'd reject the least likely character and opt for another.

A few pages further along, under "Closure," you'll find reference to another kind of platforming, which is embodied in Chekhov's *"Rifle Above the Mantelpiece"* Rule.

Plot Devices: The Deus Ex Machina

Literally, from the Latin, *god from a machine.* In ancient Greek and Roman drama, a deity brought onstage to resolve a difficult situation. In modern times the device is often in the form of an improbable character or happening that accomplishes the same thing. Or, short of resolution, the device may alter the balance of the situation. The sudden storm that results in a flood, or loss of electric power, the unexpected earthquake.

The term also describes an elaborately devised event, most

familiarly the diabolically contrived murder, which may employ mechanical devices. For my taste, the *deus ex machina* should be plat-formed long before its appearance, preferably as subtly as possible, so that while its ultimate appearance in the piece comes as a surprise, your audience will feel it *should* have been expected.

Plot Devices: Parallel Action

In movies and TV, parallel action – or cross-cutting – is another way of describing the "meanwhile" scenes. Steve Cannell, creator of *The Rockford Files*, etc., and one of the best writers in tel-evision, used to have a sign on the wall above his desk which said just that, in large letters.

WHAT ARE THE BAD GUYS DOING?

Because in an action-adventure piece (which for whatever it may be worth are known generically in TV as *Run-and-Jump Shows*), we usually checkerboard our scenes, alternating between the hero's moves, and those of the bad guys. As mentioned previously, *writing to the money* means never (or almost never) playing two scenes in a row that do not include your star, your protagonist. But in between, keep your opposition alive. What clever stuff are they plotting? What moves and counter-moves? How are they planning to achieve their ends while preventing your protagonist from reaching his or her goals? Even in literary fiction (as in "relationship" novels), such cross-cutting is essential. Obviously, choosing to write in first-person precludes the use of parallel action.

Plot Devices: The Penny-Drop

This is a device I hadn't heard of till I began writing mysteries. Briefly defined, the penny-drop is that point in your tale where some-thing significant dawns on one of your characters (commonly, the detective) – that moment-of-realization (as in the solution to the puzzle, or the solution to how to reach the solution). It's valuable in other forms besides whodunnits – where it's often the curtain line-or-incident that forms the Second Act button.

Sometimes the penny drop is triggered by something seen or heard. A word or phrase – a throwaway line uttered by one character that inadvertently causes the other to be reminded of a seemingly unrelated event or thought or observation. A piece of information that completes an equation, that causes certain earlier events or facts to connect, to suddenly make sense.

When employed in TV mystery scripts (in virtually all of them), the penny drops for the sleuth at the instant he or she hears, sees, tastes, smells, touches or otherwise experiences something which – when combined (usually mentally) with a fact or facts gleaned earlier – tells the detective that till now, everyone in the show has been following *false* leads. Suddenly, the protagonist has it *FIGURED OUT* – if not all of it, most of it – and is off-and-running in the direction of the "Gotcha" scene, leaving the other characters, and the viewers, mystified as to *what* has been put together, *how* it has been accomplished, and where he or she plans to go with it. In *Murder, She Wrote*, several bars of music (known in-house as Jessica's "Wheels-Turning Theme") typically signified such moments.

As with other such devices it's important, *even* if the penny-drop is prompted for the protagonist by some lucky accident or coincidence, that *most* of the other elements of the equation are *earned* – the result of his or her *doing*.

But if it's your bad guy putting it together (for presumably evil purposes), this is not *necessarily* a requirement. For an antagonist to stumble upon, or otherwise fortuitously acquire pieces of whatever puzzle he or she is working on is *sometimes* okay – though solving it through intellect and/or cleverness means the heavy is smarter and consequently a more formidable opponent for your put-upon protagonist.

Plot Devices: Coincidence

Chance meetings or observations, inadvertently overheard information, the photograph or TV news clip that happens to include something significant-yet-not-central to the subject. Accidental acquisition of a maguffin or other key element. The telltale clue that just happens to be eyeballed by the sleuth, and more.

Though in real life coincidences *do* occur, in fiction the pivotal kind that help protagonists – or antagonists – solve their weightier problems, have acquired a rather bad name. *But,* employed *very* selectively, they can be extremely useful tools for the fiction writer. As a guideline when it comes to TV scripts, my policy is to try to avoid them if possible, but in no case have more than one per show – *particularly* if that one contributes even in *part* to getting the protagonist to the goal-line. To some extent, it's a judgment call. In longer pieces, such as novels or theatrical plays, the writer might consider employing multiple coincidences – but for me, fewer are better. And sometimes, what appears to be a coincidence – two people showing up at the same place at the same moment – can often have its curse reduced by their reasons for getting there.

Plot Devices: Sounds

Admittedly, sound – as a device – is somewhat difficult to use, and hence rare, in narrative storytelling. But there are applications that can work. One of the traditional ways to employ sound is the kidnap victim (or variation thereof) who, though blindfolded, notes the ambient sounds at the place of captivity, or the sequence of noises encountered while being transported from one location to another. The recollection of train whistles, bells, a snippet of music, a jackhammer, a radio broadcast – that helps lead to the guilty parties.

An almost purely cinematic, but devastatingly effective use of sound occurs in the classic 1942 thriller, *Journey Into Fear* (Scr. Orson Welles & Joseph Cotten, from Eric Ambler's novel – Dir. Orson Welles & Norman Foster). The film opens on a heavyset man in a tiny, shabby room. He's in the final stages of getting dressed, to the accompaniment of a scratchy record playing on his ancient portable windup phonograph. He puts on his suitcoat, smoothes his hair, pockets a large pistol (he will turn out to be the assassin). Meanwhile, the phonograph needle has gotten stuck in a crack – the same musical phrase is being repeated – and repeated. Finally, satisfied with his appearance, he stops the phonograph, kills the light, and exits.

Later in the movie, which is set in Turkey, the harried, frightened protagonist (played by Cotten), on the run from the assassin he's never seen (though we, the audience, know what he looks like), boards a steamship that will take him across the Bosporus Strait. Cotten, at last confident that he has eluded the killer, relaxes in his cramped cabin. Which is when we, viewing the movie, are chilled to hear, coming from the adjacent stateroom, the repeating sound of the scratchy, cracked phonograph record, so indelibly identified with the assassin.

An ingenious use of parallel action, and of platforming, it's a very effective example of heightening suspense by permitting the audience to momentarily "get ahead" of the protagonist – letting us in on something the hero doesn't know. And for me one of the most dramatically striking moments *ever* achieved in a film.

Can such a device be adapted for narrative? Not easy, but again, having it your arsenal will give you an edge as a writer – and who knows what it may suggest to you down the line?

There are other Plot Devices, plus different spins on those described, and once you're conscious of them in material that you read or see, you'll more fully understand their usefulness in – all together now:

Hanging onto your audience!

The Moral Decision

That moment when one of your characters must choose between right and wrong, good or evil – or some shading between those absolutes – is a classic fictional device. And more often than not a highly dramatic one, because it requires struggle – usually *internal* conflict.

The solitary soldier whose finger is on the detonator-button, torn between preserving the life of his best friend, who is strapping the final explosive charge to the underside of the bridge – or allowing the enemy tank to cross safely, knowing that once across, many lives will be lost.

Or the ER surgeon faced with the choice of living up to his duty by saving the life of an injured serial killer whom he despises – or letting him die.

An exception to internalized conflict can occur when two or more characters are involved in such a decision, and they verbalize the probable up-and-downsides. The high-level conference table is a typical and familiar setting for such debate, but even there, the final choice is usually made by one character – the president, or another type of leader or chairperson.

The strongest, most resonant moral choices are those with which the audience can identify – those your readers can *imagine* the difficulty of facing. Life or death, or a decision that will otherwise forever alter a character's future. Sometimes it's a fork-in-the-road kind of thing – a critical change in direction. Or a judgment call that saddles a character with guilt for the rest of his or her days – and the character *knows* it upfront. Powerful stuff.

Such moral choices should, I think, be used sparingly within a single story, else the repetition weaken them. And for myself, the most interesting are those which are more typical of real-world situations – in which the options range from somewhat-to-a-lot-less than black-and-white. Or better still, where *none* of the choices is a "right" answer but rather, say, the lesser of two or more evils.

Using Research – Without Letting it Use You

In commissioning TV scripts from other writers, and then guiding them through the requisite drafts, I discovered an interesting phenomenon – and something *else* to look out for in my own writing. Researching subjects that we don't know much about can be one of the most pleasant, stimulating parts of the Process. And – because it's fun to discover arcana that delights us, and because the Internet makes it so easy to come by a lot of such material in a hurry – it's also easy – and tempting – to overuse our research.

Certain TV writers, I found, would become so enamored of the minutia they dug up while researching, say, a story about pigeon fanciers, or woolen fabric manufacturing, or forensics, etc., that they sometimes couldn't resist overloading their stories. And particularly, larding their characters' dialogue – with expository facts and detail that – instead of adding verisimilitude, actually *got in the way* of the human story they were supposed to be telling.

Is there a rule about how much is too much? No. Are there danger signs? Yes. One of those may be the realization that you're falling in love with your research, that you're giving in to your urge to teach, or somehow flaunt to your knowledge of esoterica to your audience.

A good guideline is another take on the Hitchcock Motto, paraphrased this time as: *"Research is real facts, with the dull parts left out."* You will have to be the judge of how much of your research you put into your fiction, but another point to remember is that you are *not* writing your story in order to get a good grade on your homework, or a pat on the head from Mom. You are writing to entertain, to impart the *feeling* of authenticity. Keep it spare. Keep it moving.

Closure

Okay — you're a TV writer, and the "hook" you've just pitched has piqued the buyer's interest. The next words you'll probably hear are: "Good. Where's the beginning, middle and end?"

Here, we'll address endings — the necessity of *satisfying* your audience — of giving *closure.*

By which I do *not* mean to imply that you *must* tie up all the loose ends. Though obviously, if you're writing a traditional murder mystery, or "cozy," that's largely a given. But in other forms and genres, an ambiguous conclusion to your story is often to be desired.

While I question the validity of postulating universal rules in art, there is one that (forgive what will shortly appear to be a pun) comes close to being bulletproof. Once we get this out of the way, we can think of the rest of this book as guidelines, as suggestions that can be — and often are — ignored without fatal harm to the end-product.

A number of you may already be familiar with the *Chekhov Rule*, but it's worth a brief re-statement. The great Russian playwright, Anton Chekhov, posited that as the curtain rises on a play — *if* there is a rifle on the wall (as in above the mantelpiece – or visible anywhere in the set, for that matter), by the end of the play the rifle *must* be used. Not necessarily fired — it might be employed as a club, or even a crutch, but it has got be *used* in a meaningful way. Why? Because it is a loaded (again, no pun intended) symbol. Because the audience *expects* it, is *waiting* for it.

Basically it means you *mustn't* cheat your audience. If you set them up for something, you've *got* to *deliver*. In the old, classic Western movies, the method of delivery was known as the *Obligatory Scene*. Near the top of the show, the bad guy does something terrible to the hero, and by fadeout they *had* to have another confrontation in which the hero evened, or bettered, the score. Usually by facing the villain down in the street, .44's blazing. The great directors such as John Ford and Howard Hawks, *and* their scriptwriters, knew they had to provide that kind of satisfaction.

We still do.

But, I hasten to add, that does *not* mean you should deliver the audience its satisfaction in a *predictable* way!

Similarly, say, your hero is the classic Alfred Hitchcockian, ordinary-guy-caught-in-the-situation-not-of-his-making, and he's pursued by smart, relentless bad guys who have unlimited resources and will stop at nothing to get him. If you give your protagonist a wife and child (or a similar Achilles heel), and the bad guys *don't* go after *them* in order to get to *him*, your audience will feel swindled. The wife and child *are* the rifle on the wall.

Moreover, the audience will recognize it for the plot hole it is. The subject of plot holes is covered in some detail on pages 139-141.

Let Your Characters Generate Their *Own* Stories

Another approach to coming up with stories – or developing subplots – is embodied in the *Harry McGraw* example mentioned on pages 23-24. That is, instead of starting with a detailed concept or story about how this or that takes place, and as a result something else happens, and then something else – *start* with one or more characters you've got a pretty good fix on, and imagine them in a situation that, say, will test them, will bring out certain strengths and/or weaknesses, will allow them to play out their *essential* relationship with each other. A *what-if* situation. Or – what if I were to pit this character against that character? Because then, as with the *McGraw* example, you can build your story *around* – out from – that central, or pivotal, situation. And, by developing it in that way, the characters *themselves* will help supply your overall story.

But in order to start there, you need a compelling, well-defined, *contrasting* set of characters, with distinctive, *contrasting* problems and/or goals that will *naturally* place them in conflict with each other. Flaws. Or tics. Or insecurities. Opposition. That is why, in creating a series for television, we try to devise core characters (the five or six-member "regular" cast) who are sufficiently diverse and interesting — multi-dimensional enough — that *they*, because of their built-in conflicts, will *suggest* enough stories to sustain the show over a number of years and hundreds of episodes without running out of material. There is much more about this, and how you can apply it to your fiction and even non-fiction, in the next section.

Whether we're constructing our story's ending, or an individual scene, or a "beat," what's cited above – the devices, the moral choices, the lot of it, should become part of our checklist, a kind of mental card-file that we should page through — automatically — as we write — questions that we *must* ask ourselves no matter what it is we're writing. Constantly. Self-editing.

All of it is part of the Process. Approaching your writing with purpose and organization, with your head as well as your heart. Being a grownup, while keeping the creative child in you alive.

FOUR

CREATING VIVID, MEMORABLE, *ENGAGING* CHARACTERS

Start With the *Edges*

The good news is there are a number of techniques for designing terrific characters, and endowing them with all kinds of interesting baggage — baggage that — when you're doing it right — will *give* you many of your scenes and story-moves, *because the characters will speak to you.* They will *tell* you what they would or would not do in a given situation. In effect, when your characters are well-conceived, *they will help you write their stories.*

That's when you're *really* cooking.

Where to start? Age? Gender? Occupation? Those are okay, certainly necessary, but superficial. External. And occupation or profession, unless it's inherently exciting (a Barbary Pirate, say, or cop or a thief or movie star), can tend to be a yawn. *Unless* you put it to dramatic use. In any case, your characterizations should go beneath the skin – *under* that basic "Driver's License" information. To the character's politics, likes, phobias, peeves, tics and hang-ups. And when you've done that, dig another level *deeper*. And another. All the way to the bone. And the best way to get there? The best place to start?

Start with conflicts. Again, *think* conflict. Ask yourself where the *heat* is. *Focus* on it.

What *kind* of conflicts?

Certainly, the difficulties your characters will face in achieving their primary goals. Getting there should be fraught with problems. Enemies, doubters, physical or mental limitations (both emotional and capacity-wise), conflicting responsibilities, bad weather.

What do *they need* in order to get there? Is it food? A job? Love? To be alone? Education or key-knowledge?

What do they *want*? Is their desire good for them, bad for them? Is it neurotically motivated, or based upon mistaken or false values?

Who or what is trying to prevent them from achieving that need or goal or want? That's your antagonist or one of your antagonists. It can be a wife, it can be a child, it can be a situation.

Again, drama is *people* in conflict – *characters* in conflict – with each other or with their situations or their environment. As in: a person lost, out in the cold, in the wild, trying to survive – *not* against a bad guy, but against natural enemies. *That's* conflict.

But along the path, subsidiary to the pursuit of *ultimate* objectives, there are smaller conflicts, tiny – more immediate – thwarted-aims, such as trying to end a phone call from a long-winded individual so you won't miss the outcome of the Big Game. Or winning an argument, or trying *not* to burn the toast, or spilling the coffee.

Any size conflict will do, from simple, minor frustration with one's inability to remove the cap from the Tylenol bottle, all the way to deception, mistaken judgment, to idealism, to passions such as hatred, revenge, jealousy, lust, to in-your-face rage, violence, and on and on.

I cannot *think* of a conflict that is too small to write about – or too big – nor should you. Endow your characters with your *own* minor irks and aggravations, the little, transient, nit-picky irritations you experience; a pebble in your shoe, stuff that embarrasses you, a non-functioning appliance, forgetting a name, the need to find a toilet. The too-human, self-conscious preoccupation with one's own real or imagined physical flaw, such as fat thighs or receding hairline or large nose. Or one of *my* faves, difficulty suffering fools. That one's *definitely* from my experience in the TV business.

Nor should *any* of your characters be too minor to be involved in, or provide, conflict. Even "walk-ons," such as the doorman or newsstand attendant who may only appear for a moment or two. Give each one something distinctive. Quirks, a disability, a short fuse, make him or her a massively insecure bureaucrat, or a stickler for regulations, or over-sensitive to racial-or-gender slurs. Or they're only at war with themselves.

Only at war with themselves?

That probably describes at least half of the people we know. *Internal* conflict. There is probably no more fruitful area for discovering the humanity – the identifiable-with facets of your characters – than the battles going on within their own heads. Perhaps one of them is ambivalent about succeeding. Or – plain-old *terrified* of achieving success. You *know* someone like that – we all do – the striver who tries and tries and tries – but somehow never quite makes it because events, or other people, always *seem* to conspire to mess it up. Which incidentally is almost never accidental. Usually, such people are losers because they are for varying reasons *determined* to lose. At life, in relationships, career.

Richard Nixon's almost textbook pattern from the time he was a child was to achieve, to win his mother's approval – and then screw up. He could *not* allow himself to simply win. It's why he left the White House in disgrace. *That's* an interesting trait, one that is addressed in greater depth later in this book (*The Fatally Flawed Protagonist* – pages 94-97). And by the way, long before Nixon became President, it was all there in his face – the paranoia – because in his mind the disasters were never his fault, but rather were caused by others – by his *enemies*.

Abraham Lincoln posited that by the time a man reaches the age of 50, "he's responsible for his face."

Look – I mean *really* look – at the people you know. Our faces mirror our souls, there for anyone to read – and for the artist to understand.

Yet, for all the information faces yield, they give an incomplete picture of who and/or what we are. There are hang-ups and aberrations – from obsessive-compulsive to serial killer – that are difficult-to-impossible to spot in one's appearance. For those, we need some fundamental understanding of psychology.

The modus operandi for compulsive gamblers, for instance, is that they *want* to lose. Sure, the rush is a plus, and maybe it even tops the ultimate goal, self-destruction. Isn't that what compulsive behavior is *mostly* about? Think about the people *you've* met who are their own worst enemies. Maybe they, like Richard Nixon, don't believe they *deserve* to win. That's self-conflict, and it is effective *because it's so believable.* It has *universality.* Your audience — a good part of it anyway — will *identify* — will *see themselves* or people they know in that character. All of it adds *life* to your writing. A bit deeper into this chapter are more concrete examples of common psychological problems, and some of their hows and whys.

I cannot emphasize too pointedly that, as it has been for me in my career, it is *vitally*, life-or-death important if you wish to succeed as a fiction writer *to think in terms of conflict.* To *frame your ideas* in terms of conflict. *And —* to *create your characters* in terms of *their* conflicts. What do they want, and who or what is in the way of their achieving their goals? Do the biases of those who *want* to succeed get in the way of winning?

Even if you your first creative impulse is a plot (or, for those who're squeamish about the term, "structure," or "construct"), even if you *don't* conceive your story as a set of characters, even if from the getgo you *know* the beginning, middle and end – your *next* step is *casting* your show, deciding *who* the players are, *what* they're about. Try to think of it as putting together the recipe for your character mix. A pinch of salt, some oregano, a bit of garlic to add bite, etc. Characters with whom your audience can empathize, recognize themselves.

Characters on the verge of, or *in* mid-crisis – or its *aftermath*, which is often just as traumatic – the death or near-death of someone close, or in the wake of serious injury, for instance.

But beware of serving up characters who are too similar. To expand on the food-preparation analogy, *vary* the flavors.

Avoid Flat-Out Opposites

The slob vs. the neatnik. The artist vs. the precision-freak. The freethinker vs. the tightass. Liberal vs. conservative. Jock vs. nerd. David vs. Goliath. Good vs. evil. Beauty and the Beast. Jekyll and Hyde. Familiar? Sure. With good reason. Such pairings are at the heart of how we create drama and/or comedy. But they carry with them a built-in risk — the cardboard-character syndrome.

Yes, there have been many commercially successful stories built around nothing more than the above setups. Some of them were even well-written. Some are genuine classics. Most are not. Many are little more than almost mechanical instances of incompatibility.

They're the ones in which the writer never went any deeper than the archetype.

Find the Facets

How much more interesting it becomes when we add a dimension or two to each *side* of a character. The good and not-so-good. Evil, maybe, but with a touch or two that we find appealing. Contradictions. Sometimes they take the form of surface contrast.

Consider one of the really dependable, classic symbols of pure evil: the Nazi SS Officer. In his black uniform with white piping, shiny boots and the silver death's-head on his cap, he's hard to beat for attractive villainy. *But* – would we find him *as* alluring/fascinating if he were squat and ugly? Not a chance. We're drawn to this figure because of his *physical* anomalies; he's handsome, blonde, blue-eyed, and has a great body.

And he's *vile*.

Often, though, and for me more interestingly, the contrast

within a cliché character is what lends dimension. Add a note of doubt to the SS Officer's psyche. Perhaps he's not as committed to genocide as he was a few years ago? That has possibilities, but it's still a touch flip, shallow. Now take it a step further. Ask why? Perhaps he has just discovered that his wife's grandmother on her mother's side was a Jew, making both his wife *and* his daughter Jews as well. Suddenly we have a character I'd like to know more about. Wouldn't you? It's push-pull.

Or the geek who's ambivalent about his nerdiness, or who really wants to break out, but can't. Or the jock who hates his body, his physical gifts, because he did nothing to achieve them, or because he feels he's a prisoner of his physique, that he has no choice but to live up to the role, that too much is expected of him. But — he's grown accustomed to the easy life it's given him, the coaches and agents and girls clamoring for his attention, the media coverage. Suppose for example that the reason for all of it is — he's a young pitcher who can perform this *trick*. He can throw strikes at 110 mph. Now — what happens when his arm goes dead — when suddenly, he can't do his trick anymore? When suddenly nobody regards him as special. How does he handle it? What are his inner strengths, if any? Because now he must rely on *who* he *is*, not *what* he *was*.

The moral here, unless you're writing fairy tales, is don't settle for Princes, Sleeping Beauties, Witches and Sorcerers. Only in allegorical literature are characters all one thing – all good, entirely selfish, all evil. So – if you're trying for believability, attempting to create the illusion of real life in your writing, you *must* dig until you find those other, less obvious – and *far* more interesting – facets. Create characters who consist of *more* than just a single attribute, who are more than archetypes, more dimensional than merely, say, greedy, or irascible, or logic-driven (a self-delusion if there ever was one; logic has virtually *nothing* to do with human behavior), or mean. Ask yourself *why* they are that way – find those *other* shadings – and then *write* about them. Take your character-definitions a step or two or three beyond the obvious – into gray areas, impulsiveness, incongruities (which, when-push-comes-to-shove *you* must be able to explain and justify) – and see what comes of it. You'll be pleasantly surprised.

It is more of the stuff of *good* writing.

Thrust

That's a term we use a lot in TV, about individual characters, scenes and about the story itself. It's another good word to place near the top of your self-editing list. Does this character have enough thrust? Energy? Motivation? Does that scene have enough? Or — does your story as a whole have sufficient thrust, or movement, or forward motion, to keep your audience involved and entertained?

Here we'll deal with it as it applies to characters. Unless there is a storytelling purpose served by a passive character, it's best to avoid such types. And certainly, unless that is what your story is about, your protagonist(s) and antagonist(s) should *never* be passive.

Both they, and your *writing*, should be *on the move.*

Again, in some cases passivity goes to victimhood, which is rarely very compelling because, typically, after eliciting our sympathies for the first few injustices suffered by such characters, most of us become impatient with them for not taking steps to better their situations. Passive-*aggressive*, however, is something else – an interesting complexity – which I'll expand upon later.

What about those reflective, lyrical moments so many authors love to write – the kind that run on long enough to cause readers' eyes to glaze over? Not good. Sure, believable protagonists will be prone to bouts of doubt, introspection and indecision. But limit them to moments. Keep them brief. Don't let them stop the forward motion of your story or your characters – *or* your prose.

Protagonists *cause* things to happen.

Even if it means trouble for them? *Especially* if it means trouble...

Protagonists thrive on *overcoming* trouble.

They *move* the story. They have *thrust.*

Which, by the way, is why you see so few kidnapping stories in TV or movies. We avoid them because they tend to be static. After the victim is kidnapped, he or she is stuck in one place, as are the abductors; except for, say, bickering among themselves, their stories stand still till the ransom is delivered, or until the situation is otherwise resolved. One of the few successful kidnapping stories was the feature-film comedy, *Ruthless People* (Scr. Dale Launer – Dir. Jim Abrahams, David & Jerry Zucker), in which the victim, played wonderfully by Bette Midler, undergoes a very funny character-transformation during her confinement. And, she manipulated her captors, thus significantly moving the story. Another effective kidnap story was John Fowles' fascinating novel, *The Collector*, notable more for its alternating focus (the same story told from both the kidnapper's and the victim's points-of-view) than for much movement. Though it is very difficult to make such stories work, these and other examples can – and should – serve as first-rate models.

Even successful writers, owners of impressive track-records, will occasionally make the mistake of positing characters whose engines are sluggish. And when *their* motors stall, so does our interest.

Beyond that is the phenomenon of the tired author. I have a theory about one of the probable reasons that this happens; it is, I believe, a product of what passes for winning in our culture, in our marketplace. When a writer — a novelist, say — succeeds in a certain type of story, or with a particular character or set of characters, the system demands a repeat. And then another. The public wants to read more of them. Publishers and agents want to make more money from them. So the writer is offered incentives — usually the difficult-to-resist kind such as multi-book contracts and/or large advances — to encourage the production of similar, derivative works. It's good news-bad news. In my experience, both as a reader and a writer, it is the rare author who can continue to produce on that basis without a serious — and regrettable — loss of edge, of quality. The fun tends to go out of it. It becomes a job. But I believe that most – and worst – of all, it's no longer a *challenge* for the writer.

In a way, it's what I encountered in series TV. And my own method for keeping myself interested, and my writing fresh, was largely internal, incrementally raising the mental bar. Even after writing 23 episodes of *Murder, She Wrote*, I was still trying to find a challenge for the 24th (not that the scripts for that show *ever* became easy). The goals I set for myself may have been minor, and in the end-product probably indiscernible to anyone else — nor did I always achieve them – but they were sufficient that each script was for me exciting and difficult because I was going for something – some little nuance – that I'd never tackled before. One that I wasn't certain I could pull off.

So, at the risk of coming off preachy, I urge you to *always* stretch yourself. Even if *you* have to *invent* the challenges, the self-imposed aspirations – your *own* creative momentum. I find it difficult to believe that being a one-trick pony is much fun, no matter the amounts of money thrown at you.

Speaking of challenges, what follows are some ways to ensure that your *characters* are sufficiently tested that they maintain their thrust throughout your story.

Goals – Small and Large

Give your characters *objectives* — ask yourself what they *want* — and then throw roadblocks in their paths. Even if it's not the main story you're trying to tell. *That*, on a very basic level, is drama. Without it, as I've said, your audience loses interest. And one way to insure the audience's continuing attention is to make certain the goals you give your good-guy characters are important enough – *urgent* enough – to *them*, that your audience will also *care* — and *root* for your protagonists.

A word about static characters – figures who are simply *there* because you might need them for a particular scene or chapter: they are like bores at a party – the ones *you* find uninteresting in real life. *Such figures are not interesting to your audience.* They have no place in your story – *unless* their dullness is part of a point you're making.

All of your characters should have some kind of goal, energy, drive. *Even* the dreary ones. Something they *believe* they *need*. Something that's at least important to *them*. Even the shallowest ones – such as the individual whose "need" is the latest high-end flavor-of-the-month consumer item. And *some*thing or someone should be making it difficult for them.

Should your secondary and tertiary characters have such needs and goals – even though you don't intend to make much use of them? I urge you to build such dimension into even your most minor characters – including single-scene walk-ons. Add it to their biographical paragraphs, so that it'll be in your head. You'll be pleasantly surprised by what it gives you when you write their scenes, the color and texture, the *aliveness* that it'll contribute to your story. Even a character who may have only a single line of dialogue – or none at all. I guarantee it will enrich your writing.

Make it Worth Your Characters' Time — *and* it'll be Worth Your Audience's

Another key step in developing your characters — *and* their stories — is choosing the *stakes*. What's at risk for them? Are the stakes significant enough to keep *them* motivated, to justify their actions? What will happen if they *fail* to achieve their goals? What's the penalty? What will they lose?

Obviously not *everything* need be a life-or-death matter. Except in, say, a wartime combat story, things could become monotonous if those were the only stakes. But between that extreme and a bad-hair day, there are a *lot* of gradations. *Use* them.

And keep in mind that the stakes' relative value – and even their nature – can, and often will, change during the arc of your stories — preferably escalating, becoming more intense. Because if the stakes diminish, so will your audience. An example of rising stakes might be those of a protagonist (a salesman, perhaps) whose initial concern upon arriving in town is a simple need for money, anxiety over closing a deal — but it escalates – his troubles increase;

first, he finds himself embroiled in an adulterous affair, which abruptly leads to a robbery or murder in which he is the chief suspect — and so on. The brilliant thriller movies, *True Romance* (Scr. Quentin Tarantino – Dir. Tony Scott), and *Red Rock West* (Scr. John Dahl & Rick Dahl – Dir. John Dahl) are models of the effectiveness of escalating stakes. There are numerous others in film and literature.

Getting back to the writer's role as entertainer, an even more important question to ask yourself is — are the stakes *high* enough, and are your characters sufficiently fascinating, to *seduce*, to *force* your audience to *care* about them – about the outcome? Because *that* is *your* job.

Franchises

Obviously, as stated above, not every story can, or should, involve life-or-death stakes, but those *are* the ultimate, and they are the reason for the proliferation, among dramatic television series, of what are known in that industry as "franchises."

In TV parlance a *franchise* is an occupation — a profession — that *entitles* the practitioner (usually the series protagonist), without stretching, to involve him-or-herself in other peoples' life-or-death problems. The standard franchises are doctor, lawyer, cop, fireperson. Others include lifeguard, private detective, bounty hunter, nurse, etc.

A franchise makes life relatively easy for the writers of such shows (and for the writer of a series of novels or short stories featuring a continuing protagonist) since the writers don't have to go through plot-contortions in order to justify placing their lead characters in such situations week after week. In narrative prose as well as in screenplays and teleplays, the franchise obviates – or at least mini-mizes – the need to contrive the "hiring scene." Almost nothing in TV is more tedious to write than the usually misconceived dramatic series in which a lead character – with no franchise – must in each episode routinely deal with life-or-death situations. The first fifteen-to-twenty minutes of every show must be devoted to (wasted?) *justifying* the protagonist's involvement – a process referred to in TV as "shoehorning" them into the story, trying to make it believable enough for the audience to hang in there.

Such shows usually fail, and more often than not, the problem should have been obvious going in, at the concept stage, before the project ever received a "go."

Should have been. Except that every few years one or another network – and writers who *ought* to know better – try to bring off another dramatic series about – say – a newsperson who solves crimes, or otherwise becomes instrumental in the outcome of really serious problems.

They *never* work.

Why? Because we don't *believe* them. Because even the least sophisticated audience-member understands on a gut-level that the reporter's job is that of an *observer* – a passive role – rather than that of a *participant*.

Can a short story, novel, or one-shot movie succeed with such a protagonist? Certainly. But usually only if he or she functions outside the real bounds of the profession – goes beyond passive observation by becoming a participant, perhaps as a pseudo-detective who *affects the outcome* of the story, as in the superb *All the President's Men* (Scr. William Goldman, from the book by Carl Bernstein & Bob Woodward – Dir. Alan J. Pakula). The true account of two persistent investigative reporters, Woodward and Bernstein were instrumental in bringing about the downfall and resignation of President Richard Nixon. Once the pair realized what they were onto in their story about the Watergate break-in, they did push the envelope of their franchise. But for such characters to work in a series of novels or movies, or sustain a weekly TV series, requires a *major* suspension of disbelief. How often can your heroes come even close to toppling a president?

In the early 1970's, *The China Syndrome* (Scr. Mike Gray, T.S. Cook, James Bridges – Dir. James Bridges) was a successful, topical, very exciting movie about a glitch at a fictional nuclear power plant that threatened to result in a nuclear meltdown. When the power company officials stonewall a feisty TV newswoman (portrayed by Jane Fonda), she and her crew become suspicious. They start investigating and, amid increasing tension and danger, they expose the cover-up and narrowly prevent disaster. Audiences bought it because it was so believable that those particular characters would have behaved that way.

But then, several years later, CBS broadcast a series about such a newswoman (nicely played by the edgy/attractive Helen Shaver) and her team. *Jessica Novack* (Cr. Jerry Ludwig) was yanked after 5 or 6 episodes. The problem: you can't do a nuclear meltdown 22 times per season. And trying to sell them as participants – beyond the unusual circumstance in *The China Syndrome* – was fundamentally untrue to their profession, rendering them non-believable as journalists. They were supposed to be reporters, but they came off as busybodies. Several subsequent network series about the press have similarly failed.

Moreover, in real- life, when investigative reporters uncover a crime, it then *usually* becomes a police matter, thus taking it out of the newspersons' hands.

Early in my career I served briefly as story editor on a different kind of non-franchise show. It was titled *Gavilan* (Cr. Nick Corea) an action-adventure series about a former CIA agent, played by Robert Urich, who had quit the spook business because he could no longer "distinguish the good guys from the bad guys."

Which, incidentally, and I'm *not* making this up, generated a certain amount of hate-mail from people accusing us of bad-mouthing the very organization that – in their minds, anyway – had saved our way of life from the godless commies. Go figure.

So anyway, Gavilan was finally engaged in work he loved — marine biology.

An okay premise, right?

Wrong.

Because every week, Gavilan would find himself *dragged* away from his favorite occupation so that he could rescue someone from terrible danger, vanquishing the bad guys in the bargain. And Bob, being the honest actor he was, played it straight — played the fellow who would *really* rather be in his laboratory than *reluctantly* beating up heavies, getting punched in the stomach and shot at. Oh, Gavilan got into it once he was into it, but – and here was the problem – a *weekly* television series? About a man who would rather be doing something other than what we've *got* him doing...? Uh-uh.

Remember our audience — our viewer? The person who loathes his assembly-line job, or selling nails at the hardware store, or her dialing-for-dollars gig at the telemarketing firm. Does that individual *really* want to spend an hour a week with *another* bozo who hates what he's doing, who would rather be somewhere else?

I don't think so.

Yet for a single gig, in a play, novel or screenplay, such characters offer *great* potential for protagonists.

Now, what we're talking about here is your classic *Reluctant Hero*. We've all seen them in movies. A *lot* of movies. Alfred Hitchcock built almost his entire, very successful career making films about this guy. Actors from Robert Cummings to Cary Grant to Jimmy Stewart and others played the hell out of him — the ordinary bloke thrust into a desperate, life-threatening situation not-of-his-making.

But – they *were* movies. One-shots. As are most novels with similar protagonists.

The moral? If you're trying to create a successful fictional *series* (novels, TV or films), you had damned well better design your protagonist(s) as people who are at least reasonably happy doing their jobs.

A brief sidebar about the above-mentioned *Gavilan* show, and some peculiarities of series television in general: I had been hired in mid-season because the show was in trouble. As usually happens with such ill-conceived projects, the studio or network's last-ditch salvage ploy is to throw fresh writers at them. Sometimes it works. In the case of *Gavilan*, however, I'd been there for about four weeks when the show's fundamental problem(s) – and their solutions – hit me in one of those blinding, revelatory flashes. I phoned the Executive Producer, Leonard Goldberg, and told him we had to meet right away, that I'd nailed what was wrong with the show, *and* I knew how to fix it. Ten minutes later, at MGM's Thalberg Building, in Goldberg's suite (larger than my house, it had been Louis B. Mayer's office during his reign as studio-head), I finished laying it out before Goldberg and an associate, both of whom were in excited agreement. All that was needed to ensure the show's success was to revise the concept, give the hero an *official* franchise (as in making him a willing operative of some governmental agency, or even a freelance good-guy), and then write it so that *saving people from the clutches of evildoers* was his *profession* – his *favorite* thing to do in the whole world. *That* was the ticket to making the show last for years. As we were congratulating ourselves, Goldberg's phone rang. It was NBC, canceling the show.

Interestingly, and *very* usefully, there are a *few* classic franchises that offer unique, *deliciously* sneaky benefits for the writer. Particularly if they're used as protagonists in, say, a series of novels or short stories. They are the private detective, the criminal defense lawyer and the bounty hunter. There may be others, but these are the most familiar. *Why* are these particular professions so valuable to writers of fiction? Because such characters, in the *normal pursuit* of their careers, can and do, and often *must*, lie and cheat. And sometimes bend or break laws. And still better, while they're doing it, *we* are generally rooting for them.

Theoretically at least, establishment-type series protagonists such as cops, judges and district attorneys can't do that sort of thing. Doctors can't. If they did, we'd cease being on their side. Oh, sure, there are the police detectives in procedurals such as the landmark *NYPD Blue* series (Cr. Steven Bochco and David Milch) or the detectives and prosecutors in *Law & Order* (Cr. Dick Wolf) who routinely bend the rules in order to close their cases.

But – none of *them* offer the *writer* as many possibilities for creating fun characters – because none of *them* can *routinely* scam, break-and-enter, steal, or commit the sometimes more serious crimes and/or mischief that PI's and bounty hunters get away with in order to *bring down people who are usually worse than they are.*

Which tends to explain the enduring popularity of the roguish Private Eye Genre. Part of the appeal is that such characters readily lend themselves to portrayal as good/bad, not-entirely-black-and-white, wily-yet-likable rascals. The con-artist who's *mostly* on the side of the Angels.

In crime fiction, of course, non-franchise protagonists are sometimes portrayed with great success. One of the more unconventional sub-categories of detective fiction has been exploited very effectively by, among others, master mystery writers Lawrence Block and Donald Westlake – the criminal-as-protagonist. Keller, the engaging subject of many of Block's stories, is a professional hit-man. Westlake has written a lot of wildly funny novels about a not-too-bright, only moderately successful thief, Dortmunder, and his even dimmer, bumbling cohorts. Further, writing under the pen-name Richard Stark, Westlake has produced a number of excellent novels told from the POV of a steely-nerved master thief, Parker.

Among the more traditional non-franchise *amateur* detectives are Agatha Christie's *Miss Marple* and Hammett's *The Thin Man*. But unlike Gavilan, Marple and Nick & Nora Charles *enjoyed* solving crimes, and we, the audience, shared their pleasure.

A notable example of a non-franchise TV series that thrived is *Murder, She Wrote*. While no small part of its success was the remarkable appeal of Angela Lansbury, the lead-character she so charmingly portrayed, Jessica Fletcher, was *not* a detective. She was a former schoolteacher who had become a best-selling mystery novelist. And in each show we wrote to that conceit, *while trying* to make it as easy as possible for the audience to *accept* that every week this lady would conveniently and coincidentally find herself in the vicinity of yet another homicide. Incidentally, the dynamic by which audiences accept such phenomena is known as *willing suspension of disbelief.*

Writers use it to their advantage in all forms of fiction and media – but I don't recommend pushing it in a TV series unless you're lucky enough to have a star like Lansbury.

And of course, Jessica Fletcher was a happy camper. She *loved* figuring out *who*dunnit. She found the challenge *irresistible* – she almost never debated whether to become involved. "Hiring" problems? We ignored them, rarely bothering to justify, or even question, Jessica's participation. We did it 22 times a year for 12 years, and fortunately our viewers were willing to go along with the gag, though around the production offices and sound-stages Jessica was jokingly referred to as *The Angel of Death*. In fact, we used to fantasize about doing an episode in which her arrival in a small town would send the citizens running for their lives.

Another thought we toyed with — and chuckled over — was that Jessica was *really* a serial killer, that *she* had done *all* of the murders — and managed to pin them on others.

But, wait a minute – why didn't the police in any of those 264 episodes ever think of *that*...?

The Character Bio

It is not necessary to know *everything* about each of your characters *before* you begin writing a long piece, such as a novel.

In fact, it's almost impossible. Part of the process is that the characters reveal facets of themselves to you during the course of writing their stories. That's why you should continually expand your character biographies. *Add* those fresh insights *as* they occur to you – *don't* count on remembering them the following day. Or – beyond the next four minutes. Same with new ideas for story points or twists. You know the kind. They sometimes strike at 3AM, or while you're driving or flossing your teeth – at which time you had damned well better scribble them on a notepad, or tape-record them, because they have a tendency to vanish as abruptly as they appeared.

A good habit I picked up TV, where I had a nearly one hour commute to and from the studio, was to have my audiocassette recorder on the car seat beside me. Many story notes, and whole pages of dialogue were written that way. I still pack my recorder in with my laptop, even if I'm only going away overnight.

Most of us learn early on to begin developing our characters by writing brief bios, three, four lines, more as we learn more about them. But again, it isn't enough to *only* write that they went to this school or grew up in that town, or that she's the daughter of this other character or he's the former husband of that woman. That's *information*, and yes, you must know those things, along with those prosaic "Driver's License" facts – age, height, weight and so on.

But what's *really* important to your story — and more importantly to *you* as the writer — the *key questions* you must ask yourself, and then answer *before* you start writing the actual text – and I am purposely being redundant here, as well as elsewhere – are: *what* are the lines of *conflict* between *this* character and *other* characters in the piece? Where's the *heat*? Where are the problems? The *pain*? The one-sided or mutual *abrasiveness*? What does each *want* — and is having a hard time getting? How do their goals clash with the interests of the other players? Are two or more of them pursuing the same ends? Will the achievement of one character's goal – the journey that gets him there – cost the well-being or the life of another character? Will it cost him his own soul? Will a character be required to make a moral decision, a choice between right and wrong? Or, preferably, one that isn't so absolute, one with more shadings of ambiguity.

These are the elements you should be looking for – and finding – as you develop your cast of characters. *Is* it really necessary to spell them out for yourself, to write it all down, or is it okay to simply keep them in mind? That's the choice of the individual author. I've been writing for a long time, and I'm *still* a lot more comfortable being able to *read* it. Somehow, having all those details in a place where I can easily refer to them beats the hell out of dredging my memory – most of all when I'm involved in the high-wire act of maintaining my overview of an entire novel.

The daughter — does she hate her mother or father? Does she have a difficult relationship with her brother or sister? Is she frustrated in love? Does she want to pursue a career that her parents find objectionable? Does she see herself as a victim? If she does, that's a pretty good fit with alcoholism, substance-abuse or other self-destructive patterns. Behavior that is often – as in real-life – at cross-purposes, irrational, counter-productive, outright self-punishing. Actions that seem to make little sense – till we peel away the layers of self-deception.

Is she the eldest? First children and only children tend to be achievers. And risk-takers. As do those whose siblings are *much* older. Almost *all* of the daring, highly motivated, high-achieving men who became the original astronauts in America's JFK-inspired push to the moon back in the 1960's were either only-children, or were far enough apart in age from their older and/or younger sibs to have felt like only-children.

Is your protagonist the youngest? Your readers will find it believable if he or she remains childlike – the baby. Why? Because those traits, while hardly etched in stone, are common aspects of human behavior we've all seen or experienced. Facets with which we – your audience – can readily *connect*. *That's* the stuff you must *know* about your characters, and then *use*, keeping it alive as you write. Material that will *give* you your characters' reactions, give you your scenes. And your subtext within those scenes.

Which is why, incidentally, it's so difficult to write interesting scenes between two people who are in love. Basically, you're dealing with characters who are on the same page. Simply put, people who agree with each other, who have no differences of opinion or attitude or intention, are not terribly entertaining. But – to see how that problem can be overcome – brilliantly, examine some of the great screwball-comedy movies of the 1930's and 1940's, films directed and/or written by Howard Hawks, Ernst Lubitsch or Preston Sturges. *His Girl Friday* (Scr. Charles Lederer, based on *The Front Page*, a hit play by Ben Hecht and Charles MacArthur – Dir. Howard Hawks), arguably one of the three or four funniest movies ever made, consists of edgy, high-energy, conflict-laden scenes from beginning to end. As do other masterpieces of film comedy such as *The Miracle of Morgan's Creek* and *Christmas in July*, (both of them written and directed by Preston Sturges). In my classes and seminars I often use the opening scene from *Christmas in July* as a model. In it, the audience meets two people who are obviously in love — and also in conflict. Sturges found the *edge*, and did it with such charm that we're hooked. We want to know what will happen with this couple.

From the start, as you are *creating* your characters, building their bios, *you* must find those edges.

Edges come *from* your characters — how *you* have designed them — and how you juxtapose them — the situations in which you place them – situations that provide *conflict*.

The sum and substance of all this, as stated earlier, is to *train* yourself to *think* conflict. During my television career, writers have pitched scenes to me by saying that two (or more) characters are "discussing" *X* or *Y*. My invariable reaction is to interrupt them and point out that discussions are what we see on PBS panel shows. We write *arguments* (more about *that* in the chapter on writing dialogue).

It's a *way* of thought. Again, a mindset. Take a closer look at the next successful TV sitcom or drama you view. In television, where the audience is far less captive than, say, in a theater, we *cannot afford* to do scenes without conflict (I don't think novelists or makers of theatrical movies can afford it either, but they sometimes get away with it). Do such scenes sometimes make it to the final cut of a TV series episode? Sure. But they *shouldn't*. And on my shows, they did not. The same pertains even if our audience consists of *one* – the reader of our novel or short story.

Yes, in books, theater and movies, we've all encountered those "sensitive," feelgood moments – scenes that are seemingly absent any edge or conflict. But examine the better ones closely and you'll find levels, nuances, of tension that may surprise you.

And if, after closer inspection you can't find any, it's because they did it wrong.

Okay, here's an example of a small edge: One of your characters — a young man — is a job-seeker, sitting across the desk from a woman who's interviewing him. And he's dying for a cigarette. And the woman's pack of cigarettes is right there on the desk. But it would be bad form for the young man to ask for one, so he tries to communicate his desire via body language, or a *look*, in hope of communicating his desire non-verbally so that the woman will *offer* it to him. Now – perhaps she doesn't "get" his message, or she misreads it, assumes he's coming on to her. Or she gets it, but ignores the silent communication — maybe because she finds it offensive, or because it augments her power in the situation. Whatever you make of it, that's conflict – in what might otherwise be a pretty mundane situation.

And it doesn't mean that there can't be other levels of conflict, about other matters, going on in the same scene, either underlying, or in addition to the conflict cited above. Problems that each character brought with them that day, or in that life. Moreover, all of the scene's edges may be, like the cigarette business, subtextual — *never* dealt with on the surface, in actual words or overt action. But – it may cost the applicant a job he wants badly. Who knows? Maybe the woman left the cigarettes there as a test. Maybe she doesn't like men who smoke. Or she does, is sexually attracted to them, but she wants to find out how forceful this one is; will he or won't he ask? In any case, it lends the moment, and that relationship, an extra dimension — an *entertaining* source of tension. Further, you may have no use for it beyond that scene.

But *thinking* that way, *creating* such situations – or better, allowing them to occur – will, I guarantee, bring a kind of life – and energy – to your writing that'll make it *unique*.

Attitudes and Conditions

In writing for series TV, where we have to create a lot of stories, the number of characters we must conjure up is almost exponential. And while most of them won't reappear beyond one or, at most several episodes, on the better-written shows we try to give them more than one or two dimensions – if only to see where the characters can take *us*. And one of the ways we start is by letting them have *attitudes*.

Think about the most interesting people you know. The ones that really stand out. They're not bland. They don't fade into the wall-paper. They are *vivid*. They *challenge*. They're the ones with *attitudes*.

Sometimes, attitudes can be abrasive, a source of irritation to others. That's the model that comes to mind. But it isn't *necessarily* true. As in someone who simply has an interesting perspective (read: unusual – or off-the-wall) on life – a unique, or at least fresh point-of-view. Or, the attitude is a product of a nose-zit, or the stock market, defensiveness-turned-aggressive, or some minor wrong-side-of-the-bed problem. Commonly, an attitude will manifest itself in strong opinions. Positive or negative. You know the type. Emphatic — usually verbal — about their likes and dislikes.

Usually verbal, but not always. As in the young woman whose "statement" is to become obese in order to spite an image-fixated parent. That's an example of self-defeating, self-punishing behavior – which is a *lot* more generically common – and *human* – and therefore *recognizable* to your audience – than being *direct* about expressing one's disagreements with others.

For a fiction writer, such behavior can be a useful – and unexpected – way of *dramatizing* conflict. Maybe neither of the parties understand it for what it is. Maybe a third party attempts to clarify it for one or both of them – and the explanation is heatedly rejected...

"Opinionated" people may often be intimidating *because* of their attitudes. Individuals whose outlooks and strong beliefs clash with – or bully into submission – those of others who may be less sure of themselves or are perhaps more staid – or repressed. People who *argue*, who are *passionate* about their opinions. Even about topics that may seem minor to you or to me. About movies, books, sports, a political or philosophical point, or about race, abortion, color schemes, religion, fashion, guns, or neatness.

Now, *think* about the *motivation* for such passions. What do they *say* about the people who embrace them – or are captives of them?

Maybe, as with neatness, or anal-retentiveness, it's anxiety, which can manifest itself in odd, but at the least, *characteristic* behavior.

Or, perhaps the attitude is one that your character is unaware of, such as being a control freak. Or obsessive-compulsive. Rigidity. Self-righteousness. Intellectual snobbery.

A common variant is the attitude that signifies *displacement* of emotions. One of the traditional house-numbers about individuals who are deeply politically "involved" – AKA activists – is that they often tend *not* to have lives of their own – their passions are expended on the abstraction of, say, concern for the masses, rather than on personal relationships with their spouses, their children, or others that might be close to them.

A generalization? Certainly.

Oversimple? Arguably.

Valid? Again, often enough that audiences can *identify*, can recognize themselves or someone they've known. It *rings* true.

Like so many common traits, attitudes, or conditions, these are a few jumping-off points for creating rounded, fascinating characters. From there, *where* you take it is what will make your writing your *own*.

Give one or more of *your* characters that kind of baggage, and then explore its source. See what happens, how it brings them to life — and *animates* the others, causing reactions, making them defensive or aggressive or resentful. Giving them stuff to argue with — or about.

And don't be afraid to give your *protagonist* an attitude that may be irritating to others in your cast, and even to part of your audience.

If it becomes too abrasive, too edgy, you can always moderate it, dial it down. Short of creating a lead-character that people will out-

and-out hate, it is not *nearly* as important that audiences *love* every-thing about him or her as it is essential that they *believe* them, are *fascinated* by them, *care* about them enough that they stay with your story to find out what becomes of them. Literature is full of such protagonists, leading men and women who are as exasperating as they are captivating.

And with good reason. It's difficult to imagine anything duller than a flawless, goody two-shoes central character. Unless you're writing allegory (which I *don't* recommend) or satire, "Nice" puts us to sleep.

There are physical or mental conditions, which can be espe-cially useful for walk-on, single-appearance characters, but can work for leading roles as well. Common *conditions* are allergies, a cold, hay fever, asthma, a sore foot or back or other part. A headache can work for you, or an eye infection. Or depression. A broken arm or sprained ankle can turn out to be a valuable problem, both in terms of pain and/or a resulting psychological state, but also as a physical *hindrance*, limiting the character's ability to, say, climb, or run or walk, or write. But be *wary* of these – they can easily come off as plot conveniences. And therefore, an audience turnoff.

All of which goes to your overall casting of your show, of your story. Your *character-mix*.

The TV Series Character-Mix

A brief description of the way that many of us approach the creation of a television series offers some further insights — and a kind of matrix — for how you might go about developing the cast of characters for your novel, screenplay or short story. And it should provide some reinforcement about this business of conflict.

One of the goals in conceiving a television series is that you want to create a vehicle that will run for five to seven years, because you will then have produced enough episodes (ideally 100 or more) to make an attractive package for the rerun market. That's where the creator and the studio or network producing the show earn serious profits — and the writers, directors and actors receive substantial residual, or "back-end" payments. Therefore, the creator must design a set of core-characters, usually four or five, or occasionally a few more, all of whom the mass audience will like, and care about sufficiently to invite them into their living rooms every week for at least five years.

To do that, the writer must model these characters *so that each one of them* is, with varying levels of intensity, in *running conflict* with *all* of the other characters.

That's right — *all* of them.

Certainly, most of us can recall plays, films and/or novels that contain similarly constructed casts of characters, from comedies to bodice-rippers, potboilers, all the way to epics and the classics. Most TV soaps are excellent examples. But the part that's truly *unique* to prime-time series television is that these ongoing conflicts must be *strong* enough, pointed enough, to last for five years — *yet* — *not* severe enough, not acrimonious enough, for the characters' differences to blow them apart, to cause them to walk away from each other and never speak again.

Or worse, for one of them to murder another whose contract has two years to run.

Ongoing conflicts *that are rarely, if ever, resolved.*

Fundamentally conflicting characters.

While that's the challenge in creating the character-mix for a TV series, in your novel, play, screenplay, or short story you have the freedom to make some of the conflicts *large* enough to alienate the characters.

Similarly, in laying out anything shorter than a TV series, you don't necessarily have to worry about being so open-ended, sustaining your ensemble conflicts for its entire length. In your stories, in all likelihood, *some* of your characters can and will make their peace with each other, *resolving* their differences through growth or confrontation – or death – violent or otherwise.

But – the basic approach is a good one. Again, it's part of the *mindset*.

Look for the *heat*.

And it's also true that many of the choices you'll make for your mix will — and should — be calculated to *take* you and your story where *you* want it to go. Combinations of characters/conflicts that most effectively help you make whatever point, arrive at whatever outcome, you're aiming for.

But again — it *is* a way to think, one that will help give your work unity, vitality. What I'm trying to emphasize is that when you've devised, say, a pair of characters who will interact in your piece, and you see that they have no *obvious* differences of opinion or lifestyle or attitude — where there is no *apparent* edge between them — *find* one. Or more.

Again, and as mentioned in the section about *Attitudes* (page 79), these differences need not be major. Or even rational. And they certainly don't have to be larger-than-life, a little of which – in fiction – can easily go too far. Edges that can provide wonderful conflict are often no more than those little, irritating traits that annoy the hell out of people. Think about your own relationships, about someone you know, or have met, who on some even totally *insignificant* level aggravates you:

The person who's constantly negative, a downer, the glass-half-empty type.

Or the control nut – and by the way, control comes in various shapes and guises. Stuttering, for instance, is often a control thing, a way of demanding "Shut up and *listen* to me."

And then there are controlling mothers, fathers – and children – and exhibitionists and more...

An egoist who invariably turns the conversation toward himself.

The self-important type who half-listens to what you're saying, his eyes – and attention – irritatingly on someone or something else.

The cleanliness freak.

The individual who repeats what you've just said.

Tics like these can add fascinating dimension to your characters — because they are so *human*. And because such idiosyncrasies tell us *so* much more about the characters (both offenders and offendees) than do physical descriptions or self-explaining monologues. And, their edges will *give* you moments, and even entire scenes and subplots.

Additionally, while it doesn't require a degree in psychology, it'll help if you think through, and understand, the underlying causes of such tics. You'll be surprised by how often giving one of your players such an external, possibly even superficial trait, and *then* delving beneath the surface, researching the root-cause of such behavior, will lead you to riches of characterization. Simple example: The above-cited person who repeats your words. On a one-dimensional level, it's good for a gag – an eccentricity, the causes of which aren't worth analyzing. But on another, it's a symptom of a *very* angst-ridden, probably massively insecure individual – whose anxieties, when manifested in other ways – can be useful for you elsewhere in your story. In my own writing, I think of the process as digging another level deeper, and then another.

The movies written and directed by Woody Allen can provide you with almost all of the examples of beautifully drawn neurotic behavior you'll ever need. A cautionary note, however: I'm *not* suggesting that you hang one or more of the above on *all* – or even *many* – of your characters. As with bizarrely over-the-top quirks, even such minor stuff can easily be overdone.

But selected and applied with care, saddling characters *you* create with such baggage, such dimension, is one of the keys to becoming a solid fiction writer, a *powerful* entertainer.

Naming Your Characters

Names are crucial, more I think, to the writer than to the readers, who're going to bring their own associations to the piece – people they might know who carry the same name as a fictional character. *We* writers need to be comfortable that this one really *is*, really *feels like*, a "Gregory," or that one a "Jennifer." Sometimes, in mid-story, as a character grows, I'll realize that a name I've assigned is no longer appropriate. I also find on occasion that, as with dialogue, a character will reject the name I've chosen; he may have *seemed* to be a "Matthew" when I began my story, but partway through, he tells me he's a "David," or whatever. And of course, thanks to the computer, such changes are at any point a breeze.

In naming your characters, as with most other aspects of writing, unless you're doing satire, it's a good idea to avoid the obvious.

But for me, it's equally essential that my characters' names are not too similar. I might find for instance that I have a tendency to give too many of my females names that end with an E sound: Kerry, Leslie, Jenny, etc. Easily fixed.

Another guidepost I've employed in TV writing that becomes easier to look out for, thanks to the computer, is that of avoiding multiple names that begin with the same letter (or first two letters) or sound. When I name my characters, I list them by hand on a card or sheet of paper, and then program them into my word-processor so that, along with other boilerplate items such as repeated place-names, each has a one-or-two-letter code. Examples: f=Fran, fw=Fran Wilman, np=Northport, and so on. And, per "Fran," I will then generally avoid naming a male character Frank, or even Fred.

One more hint I was given early in my career by a tough, nononsense producer is that heroes – particularly males – should always have names containing a "kuh" sound, as in Chuck, Kurt, Mark, Victor, Rex, etc., or, if not in their first names, certainly in their surnames. The idea is that it sounds rugged, harder more assertive than, say, Dale, Alan, or William. To support the premise, this producer cited such successful star leading men as Steve McQueen, Sean Connery, Gary Cooper, Michael Douglas, Jack Nicholson, Tom Cruise, etc.

Arguably worth considering, but – it's yet another breakable rule, notable violations of which include Humphrey Bogart, Errol Flynn, Mel Gibson, Paul Newman, Marlon Brando or Robert Redford. Or in mystery fiction, Sam Spade, Philip Marlowe or Perry Mason.

What all of those names *do* seem to share, however, is a kind of boldness, or at least some quality of catchiness, rhythm or poetry that makes them memorable. Which brings to mind Margaret Mitchell's classic Civil War novel, *Gone With the Wind*, with its contrasting major male protagonists: Ashley Wilkes and Rhett Butler. Those names could hardly be exchanged, so synonymous are they with the type of character to whom they were attached, the first refined-sensitive, the latter dashing and confident. And then there were the fiery Scarlett O'Hara and her gentle, very appropriately-named cousin, Melanie. Ms. Mitchell knew how to choose names that fit her characters as well as they fit the time and locale of her story. It's difficult to imagine a serious modern-day character named Rhett. *Or* Scarlett.

Give 'em Secrets

Secrets are a wonderful source of conflict. Character *A* is concealing something, and Character *B* is angered or at least resentful at being out of the loop – or is for whatever reason determined to discover or expose the secret. Conflict. And the secret(s) need not be major. Thomas Berger's wonderful comic novel, *Sneaky People*, is an excellent example of the mileage – and fun – that can be wrung from people with soiled laundry – the gag being that *every* character in his story was concealing something, from an adulterous affair to a criminal record to the mousy housewife/mother earning extra spending money by furtively authoring pornographic novels.

Characters with secrets — or those who *live* lies — are *far* more fascinating to your audience than those who are completely out front. Can lies and/or concealment be abused by writers? Yes. As with the too-often used *Withheld Information* story, described in some detail in the section on *Plot Conveniences* (page 137).

But written well, even small secrets will at least *contribute* to holding onto your audience.

This is especially true of heroes. Often, the less the audience knows about them, the better — as in the mysterious title-character,

Shane (Scr. A.B. Guthrie, Jr., from Jack Schaefer's novel – Dir. George Stevens) – or Rick, in *Casablanca*. Or almost any character portrayed on screen by the almost awesomely enigmatic Steve McQueen. But *you*, the writer, should have a handle on who he or she *is*, what the secrets are.

And on the subject of secrets, or more precisely, things left unsaid, whenever I read a story or see a movie or play in which a character is able to articulately explain his or her motives — even about the simplest acts, I rarely believe. Why? Because in my experience I've almost never met anyone who can objectively, *honestly*, explain themselves. Or is willing to do so — even *to* themselves.

Have you?

Most people — in whatever passes for real-life — cannot cite the *true* reasons why they bought a particular automobile, or item of clothing, or their choice of a romantic mate. In some cases they may know subconsciously, but do not understand on any level they can, or are willing to verbalize. In other instances they may be lying to themselves. Essentially, however, a good thumb-rule is that – as with real people – fictional characters who understand themselves should be rare — and those who can *explain* themselves should be even rarer.

Better, if you *need* a character explained, to have *another* character do it, either directly to that individual, or to a third party. An added potential benefit is that the explanation can tell us something about the explainer – something about his or her filters – what's being brought to the table.

In sum, fictional characters who have *secrets* — something they're concealing – even unconsciously – tend to be *far* more interesting than those who do not. Discover the secrets in *your* characters' lives — including those they withhold from *themselves* — and you will be that much closer to making them come alive.

Another way to accomplish that is to simply make them close-mouthed. In the chapter on dialogue I'll explore silences – as well as self-exposition – in greater depth.

Liars Play Better Than Saints

Along the same lines as the inability to explain themselves, people *lie* all the time. And that includes "honest" ones.

Often, as noted, they lie to themselves, usually because this or that truth is too painful to acknowledge.

Others are withholding, though not in a deceptive way. Sometimes we refer to it as being "guarded."

People exaggerate. It does not necessarily make them "bad." For the social animal, dishonesty — *routine* dishonesty — is an essential component of survival. We *all* lie.

A psychologist once told me that one of the most difficult challenges any of us face in our society is *being able to lie to others while remaining honest with ourselves.* This difficulty is partly due to the unrealities we're fed daily – among them such fictions as America's deep-seated national assumption that man – and his institutions – are perfectible. That somehow, if we simply introduce a regulation against objectionable behavior, citizens will stop doing it and therefore become better people. It's what causes our legislators, over and over again, to pass unenforceable laws against activities that are part of human nature, such as drug use and gambling, and then pour billions of our tax dollars into futile attempts to enforce them. And that's only part of it.

On a positive note, those same convictions – that *we* can be better, that we can *make* things better – have resulted in countless improvements in our society, from women becoming eligible to vote, to desegregation and other gains achieved by the Civil Rights movement, to Medicare, Social Security, and on and on.

Still, reality and Disneyland do not make comfortable bedfellows. Expressed another way, it is almost impossible to satirize something that is already a satire.

As a consumer society, we regularly buy into the advertising myths with which we're bombarded – that by becoming thin – or purchasing a particular brand of flashlight batteries – or a certain automobile or item of clothing – we'll have better sex lives.

We're lied to all the time.

That's usable fodder for the fiction writer.

Again, *we* lie to others about all sorts of *small* things. All the time. Call it *getting by*, or *civilized behavior*, it is nonetheless a form of lying.

Think of the material that can be gotten from the average person's mundane, seemingly routine daily misrepresentations.

We do not for instance generally tell people we encounter that their hair looks wretched, even when it does. Or that their clothes are unattractive, or that we regard them as stupid individuals. Most of us engage in those little deceptions almost every day of our lives. They should form a component of the characters you create – including the very human tendency to deceive *ourselves* by allowing such lies to become truth in our minds. As when we begin to believe that those ugly clothing fashions in the magazine ads are really handsome. Or that that individual who mangles the language is, because he graduated from a prominent university, really a bright, articulate person. Bad art is really good because an "expert" says it is, or because it fetches a high price. How many acclaimed movies or shows have you seen, or celebrated books you've read which, afterward make you wonder if you've missed something? The odds are that you have not. *Cats* (Wr. Andrew Lloyd Webber, based on T.S. Eliot's *Old Possum's Book of Practical Cats*) and *American Beauty* (Scr. Alan Ball – Dir. Sam Mendes) leap to mind as exemplars of works consisting of less then met the eye.

The story material provided by varieties of dishonesty – and it's *wonderful* grist for the fiction writer – comes as much from *our* buying into lies, and hype, as it does from the lies – and liars – themselves.

Then there are characters whose entire *lives* are lies, people who have become caught up in their *own* illusions about who they are – or wish they were – such as Blanche DuBois in Tennessee Williams' *A Streetcar Named Desire*. Or Willy Loman in Arthur Miller's *Death of a Salesman*.

Habits, Hang-ups, Hobbies and Hatreds

Other sources of conflict, of color and edge, can be found in the special interests your characters possess. What are their hobbies? Their little obsessions? And are those interests the *result* of their hang-ups, their neuroses and psychoses? Are they obsessive-compulsive? Are they paranoid? Are they anal-retentive? You can get a *lot* out of that one, above all if it's a comic character.

Self-destructiveness is another fertile area. Winners and losers. The truth, I suspect, is that *most* people are ambivalent about success, that the difference between a winner and a loser is so narrow that in a winner, perhaps only 49% of him or her wants to lose (possibly less, but 1% percent or so is really all it takes). This is expanded upon further along, in the section on *Fatally Flawed Protagonists* (page 94).

Anyway, the foregoing is a far-from-comprehensive sampling of interestingly-drawn, multilayered individuals that hopefully resonate for you. *And* you don't have to be Sigmund Freud to create characters like them. All you need to do is *look* at yourself and the people you know. Because not only are *we* walking compendia of psychological problems, so are our friends. *Use* them. Examine them. That's what friends are for.

What are their passions? What are their hates? Are they closet bigots? Are they elitists? Do they lack patience with people of a lower social station? Even heroes can – and often do – embody these imperfections, these contradictions. And they *should*. Because then they'll *breathe*. Because living people are almost never all one way or another.

And while these are things you should think about in creating your characters, understand that you won't necessarily *use* everything you give them.

But – everything you *do* know about them will inform the way you write them – will make *them* more fascinating – and make *you* a better writer.

Further, you may find that though you've written pages and pages of biographical notes, you'll only employ a fraction of it in your story. Maybe it's because you realize as you get into your narrative that one or more of the attributes you've chosen makes this-or-that-one too unwieldy, or unattractive, or too unsympathetic to be, say, your heroine. That's okay. From the top of the show, most of us aren't going to get it right anywhere *close* to a hundred percent of the time. Almost certainly not early on in your fiction writing career.

Just don't shy away from those *edges*. Fight that natural or conditioned reluctance to deal head-on with drama in your *own* life. *Let* your characters *express* their emotions. Or let them harm themselves by suppressing them.

Find the *Permutations* of Conflict

Another take on the same theme: in conceiving your character-mix, in constructing your players so that this one conflicts with that one, because of, say, jealousy, or greed, or some other attitude about this or that: leave yourself open to how those same attributes will cause him or her to interact with the *other* characters in your story — and vice-versa. Allow yourself to imagine *all* of the possible crosscurrents that can exist between them, the contrasts. Take the time to explore ways in which each of their goals and/or agendas may conflict with the *other*, more minor characters.

I find it helpful to note for myself, in each of the biographical sketches, just *how* that character conflicts with several others. It reminds me to think about it when I get into the story.

Say you've got a classic triangle, a man, a woman and the other woman. You can probably design the conflicts for that group standing on your head, but – the setup has been done to death. It needs some extra dimension. So — say you add the other woman's father? Now, he probably has an attitude about his daughter fooling around with a married man. That's additional conflict. But take it a step further. Suppose that the married man, your errant husband, *works* for the other woman's father. Perhaps the younger man is the father's protégé.

Suddenly the mix begins to vibrate with story possibilities, with potential scenes and twists, doesn't it? It begins to offer opportunities for all sorts of interesting *permutations*. The husband might "have something" on the other woman's father. The father might want the man to get a divorce and marry his daughter, so he confides to the wife about her husband's infidelity — but — she doesn't believe him. And-so-on-and-so-on.

My mentor, incidentally, referred to this sort of business with an expression that has become one of my favorites: *muzhi-muzhi*. Intrigue. Lurking-and-skulking. Moves and countermoves, their purposes not always immediately apparent.

Stuff going on.

Whether you're writing romance or action-adventure or mystery or sci-fi, *play* those relationships, those conflicts and problems. Keep up the muzhi-muzhi.

As stated, restated and now repeated again, conflicts can grow from events that happened in the past, they can result from the awkwardness of new relationships, the clash of people with differing goals.

The essence of *any* story is *people* whose desires are thwarted. One of your characters wants something and another intends to prevent him or her from achieving it. That's all.

But the second character doesn't have to be a person. It *could* be the first one's situation, environment, or alter-ego. It can be an animal.

A caveat: don't make your conflicts too similar. Vary them. If you've got a revenge motif between two characters, don't repeat the same problem between your other players. Mix them up, unless of course their resemblance is intended to make a point in your story.

Character-types: More About Heroines and Heroes

Again, give 'em *colors*. Give 'em *dimension*. As mentioned, *even* if you're writing fantasy or magic-realism or an allegory about good-versus-evil or some other symbolic situation, make your important characters *complicated*. That means including-but-not-limited-to your leading men and women. Give them weaknesses as well as strengths. Conflicts. Both internal and external. Don't make them perfect. *Give* them those tics, eccentricities. Don't be afraid to give them prejudices and/or other problems that might make them – at first glance – unattractive – and/or politically incorrect. Remember Scarlett O'Hara, who was as irritating as she was fascinating.

Perfection is boring. And difficult to believe. It's the stuff of Fairy Tales.

But again — mysterious is good. Holding stuff back is good. Enigmatic is good.

Don't *necessarily* spell it all out.

Make Your Audienc*e Cheer* For Your Protagonist

Even if you're writing an anti-hero, there must be something about that individual to make your audience *care* about the outcome.

And what*ever* you do, remember that heroes and heroines do *not* feel sorry for themselves. Oh, sometimes they might for a moment, but then they should quickly pull *themselves* out of it — as in the previously-referenced episode of *The Law & Harry McGraw*.

Or to put it another way, when was the last time you rooted for a whiny, self-pitying protagonist?

Angry — over injustices done to them? Yes. Determined to avenge a wrong? Yes. Scarlett O'Hara felt sorry for herself for maybe five minutes. And even *that* was arguably part of her manipulation-act. After that it was pure "I'm not gonna take this shit anymore."

We root for people who are *doing* something to *change* their lives, to *achieve* their goals. Even someone as self-absorbed as Scarlett.

The Fatally Flawed Protagonist

The fatal flaw is a wonderful, writer-friendly, totally believable human problem that exists in people we all know. It is a device that's been employed by writers for as far back as there have been stories — effective but somewhat overworked in parables, including but not limited to characters such as Icarus and most of the major players in the Bible. In more recent times it has been used with great success by, among others, Will Shakespeare, Herman Melville, Arthur Miller, and my favorite specialist in that type of character, John O'Hara.

Near the top of many of his novels, O'Hara would set up a tiny defect or weakness in the personality of his protagonist — and pay it off by the end, when it either destroyed his or her life, or changed it profoundly, usually not in good ways. I don't mean that they were *all* down endings, but they had a weight, an inevitability, that is for me very satisfying. That may also be why so few of his novels have been translated into movies. As mentioned, American audiences *like* sunny endings.

Eddie Felson and Julian English are another pair of such classically flawed fictional characters whose model hang-ups and psychoses are worth our study.

Eddie Felson is a paradigm winner/loser whose inconsistencies are eminently stealable. Eddie, beautifully realized by Paul Newman, was the title character in *The Hustler* (Scr. Sidney Carroll & Robert Rossen, based on the novel by Walter Tevis – Dir. Robert Rossen). It's a marvelous film in many ways, but especially in its delineation of this unique, complex, very human guy. Eddie Felson was this great pool player whose fatal flaw was nailed in a line of dialogue delivered by an observer: "You're a wonderful pool player, Eddie, but you got no character." This, as mentioned earlier, is the *right* way to handle verbal exposition.

At the beginning of the film, Eddie is arrogant, super-cool, a smartass punk who challenges the reigning pool champion, Minnesota Fats, and beats him. *But* instead of walking away a winner, Eddie keeps on playing Fats, trying to rub it in – and at the end of their marathon, all-night match, Eddie has lost – *everything*. And piece-by-piece we start to realize there's a lot more to Eddie Felson than was obvious. As Eddie's layers are revealed, we begin to understand that Eddie doesn't *really* believe he deserves success. Which of course is why, however uncomfortably, we *identify* with him. As with Melville's Captain Ahab and so many other great fictional creations, Eddie is to a greater or lesser degree *all* of us.

By the end of this memorable film, however, Eddie has become a different guy. He has experienced a rite of passage. Eddie Felson has acquired "character." That's a *wonderful* arc.

Julian English is the protagonist of what I regard as one of the five-or-ten *best* American novels, the most *perfect* novel I have ever read. The author is John O'Hara, one of the truly great American fiction writers – and *Appointment in Samarra* was his first of many novels. He also wrote extraordinary novellas and a prodigious number of superb short stories. I've read *Samarra* probably five times (Hammett's *The Maltese Falcon* is the only title I've revisited more). Julian English was indeed a character with a *fatal* flaw, a genuinely tragic figure about whom I'll say no more. Instead, I really urge you to read the novel, and to learn. And if you've never sampled O'Hara, you're in for some very nice surprises, among them his gifts for economical, energetic writing – and wonderful, character-defining dialogue.

Create a character like Richard Nixon. We cheer his success, and then we're touched by his self-imposed downfall — and along the way we feel involuntary, even slightly reluctant *compassion* for him. Mixed emotions. Why? Because he is so *universal*. Because, I suspect, there's a little-to-a-lot of him in most of us.

Or perhaps, as with Budd Schulberg's Sammy Glick (*What Makes Sammy Run?*), the flaw is more one-dimensional but no less believable – boundless, ruthless ambition.

Other fatal flaws – faith in some other false hope that ultimately destroys the believer. A romantic, perhaps? A dream-chaser? A moralist? The political activist who perhaps sacrifices personal relationships — or his life — in pursuit of impossible or unrealistic or even *worthless* goals. Doomed to disappointment, yet never recognizing the problem. Never learning the lesson. Or, in denial – refusing to *accept* it.

Cervantes' Don Quixote.

Melville's Captain Ahab.

But *beware* of the last two. In today's somewhat jaded world, they present a difficult challenge for the writer. While the character who pursues an impossible dream – or sacrifices for an ideal – has an undeniably romantic cachet, the downside is convincing your audience to buy into the romance. To *not* lose patience with the character *despite* the fact that he may arguably be a schmuck – to say "there but for good fortune go I."

The multiple award-winning movie, *A Man For All Seasons* (Scr. Robert Bolt, Constance Willis, based on Bolt's play – Dir. Fred Zinnemann) presents a case in point: The protagonist/martyr, Sir Thomas More ultimately goes to his death over his opposition to the formation of the Church of England. Despite being well-directed and powerfully played, and with lots of good dialogue, the story fails to convince me, and, I suspect, a lot of others – even in the context of Henry VIII's reign – that Sir Thomas' cause was really worth dying for. Though Bolt tried to sell us an admirable Man of Principle, his hero finally comes across as a stubborn, tightass fool.

Which very much goes to the next topic:

Attractive **Protagonists**

In the area of making sure the audience *cares* about our hero or heroine, about what *happens* to him or her, a vital question we ask ourselves in TV writing is – will a particular trait or attitude cause the viewer to *lose sympathy*?

It can be a kind of tightrope-decision: we want the characters we create to have edges, to be provocative, to have those imperfections. And yet they *must* to be likable enough to hold the audience.

But it's *so* easy to go too far in the direction of "selling" our characters, of too-obviously begging for the reader's or viewer's affection.

In commercial TV there exists an almost paranoid fear on the part of advertisers and networks of offending even the tiniest portion of the mass-audience. One of the more unfortunate by-products of this dread is a process that takes place in the final stages of readying the teleplay for production. It's known in the business as "putting the script into the <u>blander</u>." Part of which is sometimes an actual negotiation between the writer-producer and the network. Frequently this bargaining extends beyond softening character-edges, to the toning-down or removal of onscreen violence and/or sexual content. As ridiculous as it seems, I have occasionally been involved in literal dialogue-tradeoffs on the order of: "Okay, we'll give you two 'damn's' for one 'pissed-off.'" Too often the result – one we've all seen – is that too many edges are smoothed and rounded off, rendering the content so flat and the characters so excruciatingly ho-hum as to make them downright uninteresting. Unwatchable. The same dynamic sometimes occurs on certain "star-driven" shows, in which the lead-actor wields enough clout to dictate the shadings of the character he or she is portraying – and/or the choice of writers and scripts. This can prove especially detrimental if the actor in question is too worried about "image."

Eventually, if a writer is lucky, or is enough of a pain-in-the-ass – or both – he or she may reach a position where the network offers no interference at *any* stage of a show's script-development or actual production. Such was my good fortune on a few series, as well as with most of the pilots I wrote.

Not all of the interference comes directly from the networks, but *all* of it is a straight-line offshoot of the advertisers' terror. An amusing example: In most TV series, the automobiles used in the show are supplied free of charge by manufacturers who wish to showcase their vehicles. A number of years ago it became the practice on several of the action-series for the villains to drive Mercedes Benzes. A logical choice if you think about it – the brand is both expensive and no-nonsense tough-looking. It said a lot about the villains' competence.

Well, the executives at Mercedes Benz North America picked up on the trend, and interpreted the statement we were making in a different – and not entirely mistaken light – that it was in effect a kind of negative advertising message. So they mandated that they would no longer provide their automobiles to the production companies – unless the good guys drove them.

Back to the characters. Basically, the better series, as with the better movies, novels, stories and plays, present figures who are *daringly* abrasive, often *challenging* us to stay with them. Consider – from the landmark TV series *NYPD Blue* – Detective Andy Sipowicz, so beautifully played by actor Dennis Franz. Andy is irritating, argumentative, a bigot, alcoholic, conflicted, judgmental, overly guarded – while simultaneously a super detective, highly moral, a guy whose pain we *feel*. Audiences cannot take their eyes off him.

In a sense, the lesson here is to strive for that balance in your characters' yin-and-yang – those offsetting, positive/negative traits and tics. And to question your own choices about the sharpness of their edges, about how far you wish to test the limits of this likeability-offensiveness quotient.

And now we come to the creation of *another* type of character, one that carries with it the same problems, *and* is of equal or even *greater* importance than designing appealing protagonists:

Intriguing Heavies

"Listen, kid — even yer bad guys have gotta be attractive."

A knowledgeable, crusty, cigar-puffing comic-book editor gave me that priceless piece of advice very early in my career. At the time I didn't realize how memorable, or how resoundingly true it was — but it has certainly served me well, affecting *all* the fiction I've written since.

There are many good reasons actors *love* to play villains or villainesses. Near the top of the list is the fact that, when well-written, the heavy is usually the most *interesting* character in the show. Occasionally it's purely physical. Remember the Nazi SS Officer?

We're fascinated by well-conceived baddies because they *are* attractive. They have *dimension* — intelligence, or at least cleverness and, ideally, a certain amount of charm. And the more effective ones are rarely *all* bad. The result is that they're *spellbinding*.

Even more than with protagonists, there should be a push-pull about heavies that causes us to feel a sometimes-guilty ambivalence — even outright sympathy. Don Corleone, in Mario Puzo's amazing *The Godfather*, or the Don's son, Michael, or Tony Soprano of *The Sopranos* (Cr. David Chase) come to mind, as do Shakespeare's portrayal of Richard III and Bram Stoker's Count Dracula. In TV we refer to them as *Good Bad Guys*, some of course being nicer than others.

A brief-but-pointed anecdote about that, from my own experience: I was pitching a pilot idea at CBS, a notion for a World War II dramatic series. Titled *Cody's War*, it took place in 1944. Its major setting was a U.S. Army Forward Field Hospital housed in a battle-scarred French chateau in Normandy. Adjacent was a little French town with an Anthony Quinn-type mayor who had a zaftig daughter and a son in the Underground. A few kilometers east there was this more-or-less static battle-line between the Americans and the Germans who, during the course of the series would occasionally — and temporarily — retake the town and the chateau.

It had, as we say in the TV world, a lotta *stuff* going for it. Yanks, Brits, French, Nazis, life, death, medical, guy/girl, combat, the works. And Cody, the head surgeon, was this romantic/heroic type with an eye-patch. All in all we're talking good, solidly commercial, *exciting* concept.

And when I finished my pitch, the young CBS guy who made the decisions said he *really* liked the idea, but he was already developing two World War II series for next season, so — unfortunately — he had to pass. I then asked him what the other World War II shows were about. He explained that one focused on the Home Front, and the other on the war in the Pacific, against the Japanese.

Here, this little tale becomes somewhat less about writing — and a lot more about chutzpah.

Or...dumb, smartass arrogance.

Whatever it was, upon years-later reflection, I still don't know where in hell my next remark came from, but as my agent and producer were rising to leave, I said to the executive, "Have you got about five minutes? Because I'd like to explain World War II to you."

Agent and producer looked at me as if I'd lost it, but the executive grinned and told me to go ahead. And I did.

I gave him the comic-book editor statement about attractive bad guys, then added, "That's why the war against the Japanese is not commercial..." Now you have to understand that the network — this executive — had already committed to $100,000 in scripts and rewrites. He asked me to continue. And I was rolling: "...I mean as a TV show, nobody cares about the war in the Pacific – because the enemy was this bunch of little guys in scruffy-looking uniforms..." I could almost hear the agent and producer groaning, but I plunged ahead. "...But — the war against the Germans, that's another story. They were tall, blond, blue-eyed, gorgeous. And they wore these glamorous uniforms. I mean it's this really cool combination of pure evil — and beauty. You can't top it. It's why shows about the Holocaust and World War II in Europe keep getting made, and pull big numbers – but you don't see a lot of blockbusters about the war against the Japanese..." Silence.

Which I milked for a moment, then – my button: "Otherwise, how do you explain why half the Jews in New York and Beverly Hills drive Mercedes Benzes?" There was an uneasy laugh from my Jewish producer and Jewish agent, an awkward grin from the CBS executive that I read as "where the hell is *this* going?" And then I continued, explaining that I had once asked my New York shrink about this apparent anomaly, and he had described it as a very common psychological phenomenon: "identifying with the aggressor."

Another awkward silence. I added: "I mean – personally, I don't even like to *ride* in German cars, much less want to *own* one. But in Israel forgodsake there are almost nothing *but* Mercedes Benzes. Go figure..."

The CBS guy laughed, which more-or-less gave my companions permission to *sort of* laugh. We all said thanks and walked out of the office. A minute or so later, the producer and agent and myself were in the reception area doing a quick post-mortem, and the executive poked his head out, grinning, and said, "Go ahead. Write it." I had the assignment.

End of anecdote. The moral? Once in a while speaking the truth *won't* result in your being taken outside and shot.

Just don't count on it.

Oh – they never shot a pilot episode. But the script got me a *lot* of other work.

Back to creating strong antagonists.

Sometimes their strength is quickness of mind, their logic, their vision. And certainly, again, their intellect. Because beyond making your bad guys attractive, they should be *smart, resourceful.* Almost nothing weakens a story, or diminishes tension — *or* your hero — more than dumb or inept heavies. Yes, in certain types of stories, such as satires, stupid and/or incompetent bad guys can be entertaining. A few writers have raised the portrayal of comic heavies to art-form level – nobody that I know of handles it better than Donald Westlake and Elmore Leonard.

But if your intention is to create *serious, believable* challengers for your protagonist, the more formidable you make them, the greater the menace, jeopardy and suspense.

Hannibal Lecter in *Silence of the Lambs* (Scr. Ted Tally, from the novel by Thomas Harris – Dir. Jonathan Demme) was a monster who *ate* the faces of his victims, and he repelled us. *Yet* – like FBI Agent Clarice Starling, we were *drawn* to him. He is a *worthy,* wonderfully realized adversary. Parenthetically, Lecter is also a wonderful example of the difficult-to-achieve attractive psychopath.

Would *Les Miserables* (Victor Hugo) have worked as well if Inspector Javert had been a bumbler? Or would *The Fugitive* (Scr. Jeb Stuart, David Twohy – St. David Twohy, based on the TV Series; Cr. Roy Huggins – Dir. Andrew Davis) have been as compelling if Lt. Gerard (note the intentional similarity of their names — *and* stories) hadn't been such a formidable pursuer? I doubt it.

The entire premise of the long-successful, brilliantly

conceived *Columbo* TV series (Cr. William Link & Richard Levinson), reduced to one line, is: *An arrogant, brilliant, devious criminal <u>almost</u> outsmarts the <u>seemingly</u> bumbling Lt. Columbo, who is actually <u>more</u> brilliant and devious.* The show would not have worked if the killer was less-than brilliant (nor, probably, would it have endured without its quirky star, Peter Falk). And in those rare scripts where the antagonist *wasn't* all that clever, the resulting episodes were less satisfying.

Likewise, *Jack and the Beanstalk* would probably not have endured as a fable without a fearsome, pretty competent Ogre.

Bruce Lansbury, Angela's brother, for whom I was writing an episode of *Wonder Woman* (Cr. Dr. William Moulton Marston – Dev. Stanley Ralph Ross) early in my TV career, gave me another bit of marvelous, on-the-money, write-it-on-your-forehead wisdom when he critiqued my first-draft: "Your bad guys talk too much. Bad guys have thin, tight, cruel mouths, and they don't say much. Except for their aria."

I treasure that, and think about it every time I write a bad guy. And so should you. To ensure your bad guy's menace, make him a person of few words. Generally, as Lansbury pointed out, heavies who babble aren't especially scary. Think of Darth Vader, a man of frighteningly few words. Or Ian Fleming's *James Bond* antagonists — the ones who are out to rule the world. Usually they're rather terse — barking out orders to destroy their adversaries until, of course, they go into the almost obligatory aria, in which they self-justifyingly explain — with elaborately twisted logic — why they are so dedicated to their diabolical, evil deeds. I'll address this in greater detail in the chapter on Dialogue Writing.

In any case, creating capable bad guys is win-win. The more ingenious, the more highly motivated you make your antagonist, the better your protagonist *must* be in order to come out on top. This is true if you're writing a historical romance, a children's book, a literary novel, speculative fiction, or any other type of story.

How important is it to create formidable heavies? Let me cite another example – a reasonably funny, reasonably successful, yet indifferent movie that *might* have become a classic. Several years ago there appeared a political satire titled *Wag the Dog* (Scr. Hilary Henkin, David Mamet, from the novel, *American Hero*, by Larry Beinhart – Dir. Barry Levinson), which was flawed in such an amateurish way that one wonders if the professionals involved failed to realize they had a numbingly fundamental story-problem, or if was another case of Hollywood's contempt for the audience. The story which played out in *Wag the Dog* was about a group of Washington and Hollywood Insiders who, in order to distract the public from news of a Presidential scandal, set out to create a giant, elaborate fabrication – a phony European War, complete with newsreel combat footage, refugees, press coverage, etc.

A funny idea, right? And, with its topnotch cast and expert, knowing direction by Mr. Levinson, a lot of laughs.

Except that the movie didn't work *nearly* as well as it *should* have. Worse, it was *unsatisfying*. Why? For a reason so rudimentary that even the most indifferent episode of the dumbest, most pedestrian TV series – say *The Dukes of Hazzard* – would *never* have accepted it in a script, much less put into production. The script for *Wag the Dog* had a basic, fatal, virtually "Writing 101" omission.

There was *no* bad guy.

No serious antagonist, and no risk of penalty if the gag failed or the perpetrators exposed.

Which meant that the movie *had no suspense.*

Nobody was trying to stop these people from pulling off their stunt. Nobody was onto them. Unlike good fiction, or real-life, there was no antagonist – no Woodward & Bernstein, or a fanatical, self-righteous-but-dangerous sweaty-palmed Kenneth Starr-type – a *Wile E. Coyote* who *smelled* the conspiracy, who doggedly tried to expose it, only to be outwitted by the protagonists each time he thought he had them dead to rights. And so, audiences sat there watching the perpetrators simply *do* what they set out to do – fool the public, with no jeopardy, no narrow escapes along the way.

What makes the example so egregious is that it would have been ridiculously easy to remedy – and would have made the film infinitely funnier, and more importantly, audience-satisfying and *memorable.*

In defense of the filmmakers it is quite likely that they wanted to show just how easily such shenanigans can be pulled off. *But* it is basic to any dramatist's skills that the above-described fix would have made the point far more emphatically. Instead, the film was a mildly entertaining but rather limp one-joke exercise.

It is not *only* well worth your time to create *really* effective bad guys.

It is *imperative.*

Outsiders

The Outsider-protagonist (AKA *Fish Out of Water*) has broad appeal and offers a wealth of story-possibilities. As mentioned, film director Alfred Hitchcock used the device over-and-over — an ordinary man who suddenly, to his surprise/horror is thrown into a dangerous situation. In the Hitchcock canon, the hero unknowingly coming into possession of the maguffin usually triggered it. Or, as in *North By Northwest* (Scr. Ernest Lehman – Dir. Alfred Hitchcock), the ordinary guy *is* the maguffin, pursued by the heavies because they're convinced he's someone else. One of the cleverer twists in that film was that the "someone else" did not exist, but was rather, a fictional decoy set up by the good guys.

Additional Hitchcock-directed examples of the outsider-hero, though not the only ones, are *Saboteur* (Scr. Peter Viertel, Joan Harrison and Dorothy Parker, St. Alfred Hitchcock), *The 39 Steps* (Scr. Charles Bennett, Alma Reville, Add'l. Dialogue, Ian Hay, from John Buchan's novel) and *The Man Who Knew Too Much* (Scr. A.R. Rawlinson, Charles Bennett, D.B. Wyndham-Lewis, Emlyn Williams, Edwin Greenwood – St. Bennett & Wyndham-Lewis). Other movies and books that have successfully used this gag are *Marathon Man* (Scr. William Goldman, from his novel – Dir. John Schlesinger) and

Three Days of the Condor (Scr. Lorenzo Semple, Jr., David Rayfiel, from the novel *Six Days of the Condor* by James Grady – Dir. Sydney Pollack). *Condor* is for me *the* classic thriller, the best-ever of the genre, and well worth studying. Made in the early nineteen-seventies, the only things about it that are dated are the dial telephones and bell-bottom trousers.

Less melodramatic, often comedic examples include the rube in the big city, the poor person in high society, the outright impostor, such as male or female impersonator, undercover cop, a closet gay in the straight world, or vice-versa, etc.

We've all seen the fish-out-of-water story any number of times. The point is, there's a lot of fun and/or emotional color to be had with such a protagonist, male or female, comic or dramatic. And the personal attributes you give the character, the *other* conflicts, the hang-ups and defects and eccentricities, can give *your* take on it that fresh feel.

Con-Artists and Other Appealing Rascals

I have a theory about why so many of us love to read about or are otherwise fascinated by bullshitters, people who are trying to "beat the system."

I think it's because most of us, deep-down – and some of us just beneath the surface – sometimes feel that that's what *we* are doing.

Faking it.

Oh, I'm not suggesting that many of us are, or even *believe* we are, *out-and-out* frauds — but come on — what about those nagging little areas where we furtively feel we're putting one over on *them*? Or – we wonder why they haven't caught on that we're not as good as the Big Guys at whatever we're doing.

When I first began writing for TV, for instance, and was summoned to the studio to be given notes on my story outlines or first-draft teleplays, I would come away from the meetings humbled, truly wondering why they had ever hired *me*, and worse, how long it would be before the Truth was discovered – that I had been misrepresenting myself – that I had *absolutely* no gift for scriptwriting.

Understand that the staff writers were almost invariably polite, even gentle, with their criticisms and suggestions. But to me they were reminders of how little I knew. So painful were these experiences, in fact, that I needed a couple of days to recover before I could face making the edits and changes they'd requested. Because in playing the tape of the meeting, I was forced to relive the embarrassment – to hear once again about all the *dumb* mistakes my material contained. Mistakes that, in my mind, had I the faintest clue about what I was doing, would not have been there.

Fortunately, they never found me out. Either that, or by the time they were on the verge, I had actually learned enough from them so that I was no longer faking.

In any case, it's one of the reasons why I have such a soft-spot for fictional characters – as well as for real people – who feel that way. But I have similar affection for those who are overt about it, the ones who are *really* conning their way through life. And I am convinced I'm far from alone in this, that it's why the charming con-artist has such broad allure, from the PI whose *profession* it is to lie his way into someone's confidence in order to get information, to the fun of a character who feels so inadequate that he *has* to lie to almost everyone. Think George Costanza in the *Seinfeld* TV series (Cr. Larry David & Jerry Seinfeld), and how George's misrepresentations and evasions made you wince. Or the person – such as a spy or undercover cop – who must adopt another identity in order to accomplish a goal while escaping detection.

Frequently, such types also have magnetism, flamboyance, an aura of showmanship, as with a P.T. Barnum, or the bigger-than-life politician, the real estate tycoon, TV preacher or used-car salesperson. Whether they're the real thing, or really phony.

We enjoy these characters because we *identify* with them. And, I suspect that many of us vicariously *enjoy* being taken in by them, caught in their spell.

Adolph Hitler was a superstar con-man who bamboozled an entire nation. Film clips of his speeches, either silent or without understanding the words, reveal his amazing, almost hypnotic charisma.

And again, a large part of why such characters fascinate us is *because* they lie, *because* they have secrets. Because they're so flawed — such arresting, even perplexing mixtures of good and bad.

Con-artists can be *great* protagonists, wonderful heavies, or attractive secondary characters. But be careful when you use them in non-leading roles — they're liable to *steal* your show.

Just such a situation arose during my early efforts with *The Sixteenth Man*. When I first conceived it, I discovered that I had a fundamental problem. The character who quickly, clearly emerged as (for me) the most interesting was Charlie Callan, a likable, fast-talking-because-he-was-usually-in-trouble private eye (a con-man, really). The trouble was, in the linear story I was laying out I had no choice but to kill him off after the first few chapters. There seemed to be no solution, so I set the project aside for several years. Then I happened to read *Lily White*, a wonderful novel by one of my favorite writers, Susan Isaacs. In *Lily White*, Ms. Isaacs tells two parallel, intertwined stories, in *alternating* chapters, one taking place in the present and the other 30 years earlier. *And* each of the two stories had its own distinctive typeface. A deceptively simple — yet obvious — device that worked beautifully. And suddenly I realized that by emulating Ms. Isaacs' format for *Lily White*, I could keep *my* con-man alive till the end of my book.

Character Arcs

Another *essential* element of character creation is that of *arcs*. Unless you are Woody Allen, who often gets away with having his characters just as screwed up at fade-out as they were at fade-in, *your* characters — or at least the important ones — should be in a different place at the end of your story than they were at the beginning. They should, on some level, have undergone changes, profound or simple, small or large.

The question of where your characters are coming from — and where they are headed — their arcs — is one that you, the writer, need to ask — and answer — in terms of your overall story. Is this one enroute to self-knowledge? Is that one out to find God? Is another in process of realizing that money — or love — is not everything? Or learning that being true to one's self is what it's all about?

Moreover, in relation to their goals, you must decide upon which direction they're moving within each *scene*. Where they are at the beginning of the scene, and at the end.

Are they closer to finding what they're after, or further away? Because a character's movement need not always be forward. Frustration can be effective theater. As outlined earlier, it's essential drama to provide a setback or two or three along the road to the goal-line. And in longer forms, a lot more than two or three, especially for your primary storyline and your major characters. Including some that threaten abject defeat.

Forward or backward are good. Sidewise – not usually.

Remember, They Had Lives *Before* Page One

It is *crucial* to good writing — and good characterization — to keep in mind that your characters' lives did *not* start on the first page of your story, and, unless you kill them off, they won't end at the final page. They've been going on for years. They've got baggage — the type of hang-ups, prejudices, neuroses cited earlier. Stuff that *you* can — and should — invent, and dramatize. And some that you may add during the course of telling their stories.

You are in control — at least up to that wonderful point when you have realized your characters so thoroughly, when you've endowed them with all these attributes, with enough *humanity,* that they take on lives of their own. That magical moment when *they* begin to tell *you* how to write the story.

You'd better be prepared to *hear* what they have to say.

Discovering, and Then *Listening* to Your Characters

As fiction writers we frequently use people we know as models for our characters, or, as suggested earlier, we might base one or more of them on real-life public figures. The following example of my own search for the *character* of a real, historical figure may be one you'll never encounter on a one-to-one basis, but it is *all* about discovering, and *listening* to your characters. And though I learned it while writing for the stage rather than TV, it will, I promise, give you something to chew on – something you can *use*, no matter your medium or style.

A number of years ago, I had a vision for an opera about John F. Kennedy. I decided to try to write it, and began researching his life, reading biographies and recollections of the man and his times, both critical and admiring. I took on a collaborator, lyricist/composer Will Holt, and together we started to build on what I had begun. Will, too, immersed himself in books about JFK, and it soon became apparent to him, as it already had to me, that despite everything that was known about Jack Kennedy – all the stuff that was a matter of record about his public persona, as well as the anecdotes of people who knew him, the *real* person was *maddeningly* elusive.

Oh, we had *facts*. Lots of them, but in total, they were surface. Particularly when it came to putting words – *other* than his recorded public utterances – into his mouth. Our Jack – the equivalent of a fictional creation for whom we would have to write invented-but-*true-to-character* lyrics – was a *mystery*.

We knew that Jack was the second of nine children, that his older brother, Joseph P. Kennedy, Jr. was, almost from birth, the Anointed One, designated by their father to someday become the first Catholic President of the U.S. The books also told us that in Jack's early years he was chronically ill, that as he grew, he became something of a playboy, that unlike Joe, who was a bit of a grind, he was an indifferent student. And of course, the womanizing by all four boys, urged on by their father. There was Jack's romance with a married woman while he was stationed in Washington, D.C. during WWII, a liaison reputedly broken up by the father, who feared that if it leaked to the press, it might damage Joe's future political career.

Along with all of that, there were the historical contradictions and anomalies: After Joe was killed in action in WWII, Jack entered politics – apparently at his father's behest – and eventually became President, the Jack Kennedy we came to know as charismatic, focused and highly intelligent.

But ironically, the way we, as writers, finally discovered *who* John F. Kennedy was, *and* what the *show* was about, was from something that is *left out* of *every* biography ever written about him.

This anecdote, by the way, is also about tenacity, about hanging onto your dream. Because the time that passed from starting *JACK*, until we made this key revelation was *eight* years.

Here's how it happened.

Will and I had worked our way through much of the first act, covering the drama, the conflicts of Jack's life from about age 17 through his early 20's. Early scenes moved back-and-forth through time, dealing with Jack's relationship with brother Joe, flashing back to the father's days at Harvard, and then, prior to WWII, when FDR appointed Joseph P. Kennedy, Sr. Ambassador to the Court of St. James's, the family's move to England. We addressed the brothers' participation in the war, Jack in the Pacific, Joe, Jr. in the European Theater, where he was killed while flying a bombing mission. The Ambassador receives the devastating news and it tears him apart.

We were then at the point in our story – chronicled in *all* of the books – when the father, still devastated by Joe, Jr.'s death, tells Jack that he wants the young veteran to run for Congress. The 11th Congressional District seat that, according to the father's plan, Joe would have sought.

We *knew* that for our show, we had to *play* that scene. It was too pivotal a moment in Jack's life to finesse, to simply gloss over.

And yet, in *none* of the history books is there a record, or even a description, of the scene – where it took place, the specifics of what was said. Only an arm's length, basically one-line statement: Joseph

P. Kennedy, Sr. tells Jack he wants him to run. Followed, in *all* of the books, by descriptions of Jack on the campaign trail.

The historians and biographers all made the same logical assumption – Jack said okay, and then ran for the House of Representatives.

In *all* of the books.

And *that's* when it happened for us as writers.

Because *our* Jack Kennedy said "No."

That's right. Jack – the Jack whom we had been positing from all the little bits and clues in our years of research – *told us* that he had flat-out refused to obey his father.

Our Jack had, almost without our realizing it, taken on a life. We had *found* the character.

The *same* thing that happens when one is writing *fiction*.

The pieces. They'd been there all along.

Jack's frequent childhood illnesses. One doesn't have to be Jung or Freud to recognize that as a classic plea for love and attention from a kid for whom it was made clear from the getgo that he was number two.

And the dropout/playboy business? Totally consistent with a young man who, recognizing that there was no gain in trying to compete with his Crown Prince older-brother-the-grind, chose the opposite path.

The books, as mentioned above, also described Jack's romance with the married woman while he was a young Naval Officer in D.C. And some depicted in detail the father's enlisting the help of J. Edgar Hoover and the FBI in order to break up the affair (including the bugging of their hotel room). Could it be that Jack *knew* – or at least suspected – what his dad had done?

And there was Jack's avowed ambition to become a journalist after the war. Again, a way to avoid comparison with Joe, Jr.

There were other clues that began snapping into place. We'd reached that stage where we were hitting ourselves upside the head, those "Why didn't we see *that* before?" moments – I think of it as the buzzing of the fiction-writer's shit-detector. The totality of which only cemented our *certainty* that there was *no way* that Jack would have agreed to run.

And yet – *he did*. And he won the election. And went on to the Presidency.

So, we asked ourselves, what *actually* happened?

Our answer yielded two vital, powerful scenes. The first of them, truly gut-wrenching, follows the Ambassador's touching solo lament about his son's death. Jack, one-on-one with his father, tries to cheer him up – and is rudely rebuffed. Then, the older man's eyes narrow, and he tells Jack (keep in mind that this is entirely sung) to run. Jack rejects the idea, and in a truly operatic duet – the father *demands* to know why. Jack replies: "Dad, I'm not Joe." They argue. The tension – and passion – rises, till finally Jack flatly, unequivocally refuses. His father regards him for a moment, then says, with disappointment and contempt: "I know – you're not Joe…"

And with that, the older man exits, leaving Jack alone on the stage, crushed. And the audience wiped out along with him.

Of course, we *had* to play the resolution. What or who changed Jack's mind, convinced him to run for office? From what we knew of the family, it could *only* have been one person. His mother, Rose. Which gave us our next moment in the show – Rose persuading her son that it's his duty to make peoples' lives better, a responsibility that goes with being a Kennedy. The First Act concludes with Jack campaigning.

No one will *ever* know for certain what actually took place back then – none of the long-dead players left any public, known account. But I'm convinced that we got it *very* close to right.

Closer than *any* of the biographies and history books…

More than that, however, it gave us the *spine* for the whole show – the conflict between Jack Kennedy and his father. And it demonstrates the importance of *listening*, of *hearing* subtext, of digging beneath the surfaces of your characters, whether fictional or real, no matter what you're writing.

Character Traps

One of the keys to writing *any* kind of gripping fiction, which I'm sure is elementary to most of you, is this: *catch one or more of your characters at a crisis point – a life-changing moment.* They're on the verge of something. Good or bad. Positive or not. Or something momentous has just occurred. That's pretty much the classic approach.

But in heightening your drama or comedy in those ways, be on guard against falling into the trap of creating cliché characters. The dumb cop, the sympathetic bartender, the aged-but-kindly stage-door-man, the seething nerd, the ambitious, stage-struck wannabe actress, the hooker-with-a-heart-of-gold. And on and on. You know the types. You know them because they *are* hackneyed, because you've *seen* them repeatedly. And worse than simply having started with a cliché, such characters will usually *only* take you in the direction of more clichés. Story-clichés. Predictability.

The *Obvious*.

Traps.

Of course, true originality is almost impossible to achieve – but freshness is both possible – and – not *just* desirable – it is *essential*.

In television we have a phrase for the Obvious: *"on-the-nose"* (in marking-up scripts we abbreviate it to *"OTN,"* and we use it to describe obvious dialogue as well — more on that later).

It's worth remembering, however, that every cliché was once someone's original creation. Dashiell Hammett's Sam Spade is the prototype for virtually every private eye that has followed. Before Spade, it was Sherlock Holmes. *The Godfather* is an example of an innovative take on familiar stereotypes that have since become, them-selves, cliché. Until David Chase gave them a fresh spin in *The Sopranos*. Emily Bronte's *Jane Eyre* is the basis for the Gothic Heroine, and the novel itself the blueprint for those written since, from Daphne DuMaurier's *Rebecca* to countless potboilers.

Admittedly, an element of cliché is sometimes desirable, a kind of shorthand for the audience. It used to be said of Rogers & Hammerstein's incredibly popular string of Broadway musicals – as a kind of left-handed compliment – that they were "not only original, but familiar." This can also apply to creating characters who will only appear in a single episode of a television series. There is usually not enough time to give them much more than one or two dimensions, so we try to achieve a spin that renders them fresh, though not *too* difficult to recognize. But in longer-forms, such as novels, even your most minor characters should be fleshed-out – and, if only in small ways, surprising – *inventively* designed.

Again, even if you don't *use* all of it.

In any case, stereotypes are something every writer should think about, be aware of. And when you recognize that you're creating a cliché character, ask yourself if it's *really* what you want to do. *Does* the familiar character add to your story, or cheapen it? If it isn't adding anything, change it.

One way to approach that kind of change is to stand the familiar on its ear.

Try flipping the card. The hooker who, when push comes to shove is really a greedy, selfish pain-in-the-ass. The seemingly good-hearted cop who is really a closet sadist, or has a less-extreme weakness or compulsion such as a gambling problem, or he becomes ill at the sight of blood, or dead people. I once knew an NYPD detective who had to transfer out of Homicide for that reason, a gag I've used once or twice in my writing. Or – his wife batters *him*. The goal is to make at least some aspect(s) of your characters *seem* new. Make them *less predictable*.

As said, and said again, all this is *really* about entertaining. About fascinating, and then holding, your audience.

Making *All* of Your Characters *Count*

Back to minor characters, and how to make them *vital*: think about the problems this one's having at home, at work, the insult that one may have suffered earlier in the day. She's late with the rent, or he has a blister on a toe, or constipation. A *condition*. It can be a back-ache, depression, a chronic cough. It can be hay fever, causing him to sneeze, and the major character who encounters him is a germ freak. Or it's her allergy to the cat-hairs on the major character's sleeve. Or defensiveness about some real-or-imagined personal defect – fat thighs, receding hairline, crooked nose.

When you start thinking that way, your minor characters — and their scenes — will instantly become more interesting, taking on — at the very least — *color*, and as a bonus, giving the moments an *entertaining* dynamic beyond whatever plot-advancing requirement caused you to write the transaction in the first place.

Suppose for instance that a scene, a story-point that you *need* to play, places your protagonist at a magazine stand so that – for plot-purposes – he can happen to notice a person or an event. So, rather than simply having him standing there, you decide to have him purchase a pack of cigarettes. Not, in itself, very interesting. Now, suppose that the store cashier is irritable – or has hives, or a migraine – because she's anticipating that when she gets home, her mother-in-law will have arrived for a three-week stay in her tiny apartment. Suddenly, your protagonist's interaction with her can become a challenge, *entertaining. Distracting.* So that, when he finally notices what your story requires him to notice, when your scene finally pays off, you will have gotten there in an *interesting* way – with or without going into the details of her malaise. What's important is that *you've* taken the time to imagine them.

Making the ordinary *extra*ordinary is a large part of what good writing is all about.

The *point*, however redundant, is key: don't "toss off" your most minor characters because they merely serve a necessary function in your story, or only appear for a moment. If a character "makes the cut" and ends up *in* your manuscript, make *use* of him or her.

Write them *fascinating*. Write them theatrical. Write them bigger than life. Possibly funny, or with hang-ups – or both. Pattern them after people with whom *you've* interacted — the clerk at your local food market, the person who cuts your hair, the driver of the UPS truck in your area. You'll discover that they lend invaluable texture and excitement to your story, making your scenes — *and* your writing — special.

Can your writing have *too* much of this kind of color? Sure.

How will you know? When your supporting characters begin stealing scenes from your protagonists. When the scenes start to be about them, rather than what they *should* be about.

Some Characterization House-Numbers

The following are a few common, outward, obvious traits – some of their side effects – and some general, *writer-useful* below-the-surface reasons for them. Several of the characteristics, and their causes, will overlap, or mirror some already mentioned, or to be touched on further along. The list is in no way complete, but it will, I hope, provide a few jumping-off places – and spark an idea or two.

Anger

Very often, anger results from depression or sadness, causing the person to lash out – or sometimes, lash *inward* (with many such troubled individuals it goes in both directions), as in self-punishment – from overeating to drug-use to nail-biting (which is – literally – chewing on oneself), all the way to committing anti-social acts and/or screwing up valued relationships.

In creating your angry character, or any other type, ask yourself what those symptoms may be about. Where did they start? Knowing the answers will give you all sorts of dimension to play with, telling you how they'll react in various situations. *And* – it'll make your characters and your writing exponentially more interesting.

If it's sadness causing the anger – what's the source? It might be loss of a loved one, or of one's abilities, or livelihood. Unrealized ambition. Or it could be some imagined slight. Because with People, we're not necessarily talking rational behavior. Much of the time, quite the opposite.

But valid or not – sensible or not – there are *always* reasons – which total out to grist for the fiction writer.

Similarly, illness, either chronic or periodic (as in the Common Cold) can result from anger-turned-inward, as well as from self-pity, or as a plea for attention and/or love. Resentment brought on by jealousy, for instance.

Self-pity is another manifestation and/or cause of anger. Again, feeling sorry for oneself is a form of resentment – the have-not, the loser (really or imagined).

Passive-Aggressive

Previously, I touched on passive-aggressive behavior. A way of venting anger, it's an amazingly common trait in a culture such as ours, which frowns on expressing "unseemly" emotions. Basically, it is the acting-out of suppressed anger – through some sort of punishing behavior toward another – without admitting one's anger to that party – and often without admitting it to one's self. The hostile action(s) may be obvious, even physical, or sneaky – so simple or minor that it might be regarded (and even excused) as "thoughtlessness."

It isn't.

An interesting variant is the individual who's playing a game in which only he or she knows the rules – *or* that it's a game in the first place – who then becomes angry at another person for unknowingly violating the rules.

Then there's the person who, say, repeatedly violates the ethics of a particular relationship – without admitting, or even recognizing – having done so.

Passive-aggression can be essentially defined as a confrontation-avoiding (sometimes convolutedly indirect) expression of anger. It's also a very toxic, non-healthy way. Which probably describes at least several of your friends or relatives (not *you*, of course).

Again, a fascinating, *human* hang-up.

Control

We've all encountered people who need to manipulate others. Why?

How about paranoia? An inability to trust. Mostly, it's fear.

Of failure, for example. If, in a collaborative venture, an individual can't trust others, it follows that he'll be unwilling to delegate responsibility.

But in terms of relationships, control can also provide a way of minimizing risk. A way of obtaining repeated confirmation that another person really *cares*.

Which goes to various forms of resistance to change. In Luddite behavior, for instance, an individual might refuse to keep up with modern means of communication (fax, Email, celphone, answering machine, etc.). That's a form of control – of telling others that if they wish to maintain the relationship, they have to go that extra mile and put up with those – or other – annoying quirks. In simple, it's about testing others' love.

Such a character is not going to be happy in situations that don't allow for much control. From communal activities such as parties to – say – being a passenger. People who need tranquilizers in order to fly on a commercial airline often have control issues.

A sidebar: for this, or almost any other unconscious trait, the person will likely have constructed an elaborate explanation for it – which will usually be at least 90% self-deluding.

Good material.

Hunger for Approval

Often, the person who tells lies does so as a way of winning praise. As does the character who may be terrified of failure, or is otherwise massively insecure. It's an interesting kind of desperation. There's also an element of control, of manipulation, with such people. Commonly they are trying to *manage* the impression they make on others. They also tend to be rigid, intolerant and/or judgmental.

Another way of winning approval is through excessive loyalty. The individual ignoring his or her own requirements in favor of others, even to the point of inflicting self-harm, sometimes demonstrates this.

This last also applies to the martyr-complex, which frequently drives the

Caretaker

The character who's convinced he's indispensable. Or selfless. Consider that word. Selfless. *Without* self. A character who gives up identity. The earth mother. The super-responsible person. The one who looks for, and then helps "victims." This includes co-dependency, and also goes to fear of abandonment and/or rejection.

These, by the way, are not necessarily "bad" people. But they *are* interesting – in ways that folks who have it together are not. In no small part because the former contain elements of unbalance – of *edge*. Looked at differently, just plain folks who are conventional, well-integrated members of society are not especially attention-grabbing as fictional characters *because* they're so straight – because they lack inner conflict – which generally fuels outer conflict. They are absent the problems that add up to drama.

Unless we, as writers, dig to find them.

Because in the real world – as in well written fiction – there is *always* something fascinating going on beneath even the most placid surface.

Low Self-Esteem

This can manifest itself in fear of failure or rejection, as well as in an obsessive need for self-perfection, often a product of feeling inadequate. Sexual promiscuity is another possible result of disrespecting oneself. It can be, for male or female, a way of buying approval – as well as – in many cases – repeated reassurance of one's low self-worth (as in: How good can I be if nobody will commit to me?). Lack of self-esteem can also cause a person to withdraw, either by becoming non-assertive or, sometimes, isolated. Commonly, it shows up in fear of authority figures. And guilt.

Psychopaths and Sociopaths

Crazies. Occasionally useful as characters, as mentioned previously I personally find them to be of limited interest and use because they *are* so difficult to relate to. Certainly, psychopaths have value as – say – serial killers, firebugs, or other unreasoning forces, but because of their insidiousness, their almost symbolic, cartoon-like evil-without-redeeming-qualities, their stories tend to be unsatisfying except for their potential in battle-of-wits adventures with your hero. They're uninteresting for the same reasons that psychologists and psychiatrists shun them – they're incurable. Incapable of change. Thus, written with honesty, their stories offer little or no possibility of redemptive arcs.

Unless, of course, the writer – or your protagonist – can find a way to use such a character's antisocial behavior to achieve a desired goal.

Sociopaths, who are similarly incurable, offer somewhat broader potential for the fiction writer, partly because they're such dependable sources of conflict for your other, less seriously flawed characters. Classically, the sociopath, or pathological liar, is a physically attractive person who is *unable* to tell the truth, incapable of distinguishing right from wrong. Usually charming, in most cases such individuals were/are overprotected by parents who may also have a severely limited grasp on reality. The one with whom I was acquainted was, the closest I have ever been to what might be described as "truly evil," in that he was unreachable by me in terms of getting him to acknowledge, or even comprehend his dishonesty. Such characters are rarely dealt with in any but horror fiction, probably because the outcome of their stories is usually a downer that, in America anyway, is not terribly commercial.

On the plus side, sociopaths' almost sure-fire penchant for disrupting the lives of others, for *triggering* strong reactions, makes them useful as secondary bad guys, though their inability to look into themselves renders them – like their more lethal counterparts – less attractive as first-line heavies.

The 1941 thriller movie, *Suspicion* (Scr. Samson Raphaelson, Joan Harrison, Alma Reville, from Frances Iles' novel, *Before the Fact* – Dir. Alfred Hitchcock), is an interesting exception, one of the few non-fright films to feature such a character. In it, Cary Grant played a totally disarming liar who may or may not have been a serial killer. Hitchcock intended to end the film with Grant about to murder his co-star, Joan Fontaine – a daring, and audience-upsetting climax. Instead, the studio — and the movie "code" of that era — forced a "happy," and ultimately false ending to this otherwise superb film, telling us that Grant was innocent, really a nice guy, really in love with Fontaine.

Similarly, for *Murder, She Wrote* it occurred to me that it would be intriguing to pit the series protagonist, Jessica Fletcher, against such an individual. The earlier-referenced pathological liar with whom I'd been involved became, once I'd put some distance between him and myself, an interesting model for me, challenging to bring off as a fictional character. For my script, I posited my liar as an otherwise attractive young woman whose dishonesty has damaged, infuriated and alienated Jessica. The young woman then becomes a dead-bang murder-suspect whose innocence Jessica reluctantly-but-out-of-her-sense-of-justice tries to prove. I thought it would be interesting to see Jessica torn between her animus and her belief in doing the right thing. I cite this not only as an instance of stealing a story from my own experience, but also as a near-definitive sample of the *what-if?* school of brainstorming.

The resulting episode, *Dead to Rights*, turned out rather well, affording several "fireworks" scenes for Angela Lansbury. The downside for me, ironically, was in the dictates of commercial television — the requirement for a feelgood, ultimately dishonest ending (as in *Suspicion*). In this case, our liar, cleared of the murder (Jessica having unmasked the real killer), sees the error of her ways, is regretful about her lying, and has entered therapy, presumably enroute to a cure.

Win some, lose some.

I sympathized with Hitchcock. And though, truth be told,

because of its "darkness," its usually single dimension, psychopathology and/or the supernatural are for me not all that appealing as story material, it continues to be wonderful, immensely popular grist for storytellers, from Mary Shelley (*Frankenstein*) to Bram Stoker to Thomas Harris, Anne Rice and many others.

The foregoing are a few of the many character traits – and some of their underlying causes – that are out there, all around us, as well as in ourselves, *all* of them fuel for our work as fiction writers. Types our audiences will connect with, because *in* those characters they'll recognize themselves or others.

But – those attributes and their causes can – and *ought to* be regarded as just a start. Especially if you're designing a major character. Because then, you as the writer should try for still another dimension, and another.

One way is by asking yourself what such a character "gets" from the trait. Because all of it, *each* of these very human quirks and tics are part of a *transaction*. A trade-off.

It may be that if an individual is angry at others, it's about blaming them for personal problems – thus getting rid of responsibility for his or her situation. Same with blaming "the system." Martyrdom is often a method of winning the love or admiration of others. As, frequently, is charity. Sadness, a way of buying sympathy and attention.

And on it goes. It's about thinking your characters *through*. About *not* settling for stereotypes. And yes, looked at another way, damned if it isn't about *conflict*. In the foregoing cases, largely internal.

By now it may have hit you that with the exception of sociopaths and psychopaths none of these problems suggest their owners are "crazy." Odd, maybe. Colorful, potentially. Distinctive, hopefully. Though obviously various psychopathologies will include one or more of such traits – carried to extremes – the focus here is on the creation of everyday, imperfect characters. The kinds of people most of us write about, most of the time.

The *Really* Hard Part – Or –
What *Should* Be The Hardest Part:
Introducing Your Characters to Your Audience

Okay, you've done the work, given your character-mix a lot of thought, created some great, fascinating, complex, conflicted-and-conflicting individuals — and you're beginning to *know* them. Now comes what I regard as one of the most *critical* parts of the writing process — of *good* writing. *The First Meeting* between your audience and *each* of your characters.

Again, a lesson that travels well from television writing to other forms: the *need* to hit *precisely* the right note the first time I show a character to my guy with the beer-and-clicker in his hands.

For me, one of the toughest parts of writing is in the choices I make for how to introduce my characters. If it's easy for you, you're probably far too talented and/or experienced to be bothering with this book.

Or – you're kidding yourself.

For starters, in the best-of-all-worlds, I try to introduce my characters in situations that *show* them *doing* whatever it is they *do*. An attorney should *if possible* be serving in that capacity when first we see him or her. A cop likewise (particularly a plainclothes cop). Or a doctor. Or a teacher. Or auto mechanic. Why? Partly of course, it's about first-impressions, but the best thing about catching them at a time when they're practicing their trade is that you don't have to have them, or someone else in your piece, *talk* about it.

It's not always possible to write it that way, but in TV and film (and it *definitely* carries over to narrative) the *house-number* (which, as with much that's in this book, bears repeating – and *will* be repeated) is don't *tell* it — *show* it.

And – setting that goal for yourself, and achieving it, will yield a *very* worthwhile result. Because more often than not, by eliminating those tedious expository scenes we've all squirmed through in the work of other writers, you will get your story moving more quickly, more briskly.

Further, and for me perhaps best of all, it will rid you of the temptation to write icky dialogue lines such as:

"As my lawyer, what would you say about...?"

Now – I do *not* mean that if a character is, say, a wife-beater, or an intellectual giant, or has some sort of quirk that only reveals itself under certain conditions, that that needs to be fully illustrated on first meeting. As you will note further along, misdirection and gradual revelation of character is a technique essential to good storytelling.

Okay, how do we lay in the fact that someone's, say, a lawyer? Obvious way — put the character in the courtroom, pleading a case — or in a law office with a client. But that's not always appropriate – or even possible – for the story you're trying to tell, and forcing it is — forcing it. There are almost always other ways. Some are addressed in the following section, *Exposition*. And further along, in the section titled *Kicking it Off* (page 164), I refer to the opening scenes of several movies which are worth studying for the astonishing amount of information they convey – with even *more* astonishing economy – all of it done in such an entertaining manner that you're almost unaware, until you think about it, that it's exposition.

In my own writing, while I devote an inordinate amount of thought and care and energy to introducing my characters — *especially* those who are key — again, I try to give full shrift to intros of even the minor, micro-dimensional players.

You should, too.

As with most aspects of the storytelling biz, the good writers make it look easy.

Why is it so vital to choose that singular chord — and then to hit it? Because, exactly as in real-life first-meetings, we instantly, unconsciously process *thousands* of bits of information about the other person. Messages — communicated by such things as body language — facial expression, eyes, posture. How they're dressed — the necktie-knot askew, the frayed or too-tight collar. Tone of voice, hair, excessive makeup and so on — *all* of it *tells* us *about* the person.

My father used to call them snap-judgments, and he taught me to mistrust them. Well, that may be valid when you're twelve years old, but I believe that once one has lived for awhile, once we *know* who *we* are, and are thus better able to read *other* people, such first-impressions *should* be trusted (which doesn't mean they're *always* correct). And certainly, as readers or audience-members, *that's* what we do when encountering a new figure in a novel or in the visual media. That's how we form our *relationships* with characters that authors present to us.

Are we sometimes fooled by real-life first-meetings? Of course. And as writers, we can and should occasionally take advantage of that — by employing misdirection. By allowing a character to misread another. Or by deceiving our audience.

The difference between fiction writing and real-life — in this case at least — is that we — as the writers — have a *lot* of control over what is communicated. Not *absolute* control — because everybody in your audience absorbs and interprets such information through their own set of filters. But that's true of art in general. Near the end of this book, in the section titled *The Rorschach View*, I expand on the notion that no two people looking at the *Mona Lisa*, or reading *Crime and Punishment*, or watching an episode of *The Sopranos*, are seeing the same thing, the same way. There are almost no Universal Buttons that we can push.

A few that come close, incidentally, are in the area of startling or frightening an audience; almost everyone can be caused to levitate out of a theater seat by a particularly scary, well-executed cut in a film, as when the shark first appears in *Jaws* (Scr. Peter Benchley, Carl Gottlieb, Howard Sackler, from Benchley's novel – Dir. Steven Spielberg). And *all* readers of Richard Condon's marvelous thriller, *The Manchurian Candidate* will find themselves frantically backtracking through the book, the moment that protagonist Raymond Shaw's mother shows up dressed as the Queen of Spades – because Condon has just played the niftiest literary trick I've ever encountered in print (more about this on page 144).

Such instances, however, are truly rare. So rare and difficult to bring off, as a matter of fact, that many years ago the British Film Institute produced a fascinating twenty minute film devoted entirely to the analysis, frame-by-frame, 24th-of-a-second-by-24th-of-a-second, of *one* such stunning cut in the 1946 classic, *Great Expectations* (Scr. David Lean, Ronald Neame, Anthony Havelock-Allan, Cecil McGivern, Kay Walsh, from the novel by Charles Dickens – Dir. David Lean). The cut: the first reveal of the convict, Abel Magwitch, when he frightens the daylights out of young Pip — *and* the audience — in the wonderful graveyard scene. It is right up there with the earlier-referenced moment in *Journey Into Fear*.

But — guaranteeing the same-size *laugh* on the same cue *from different audiences*? Maybe sometimes – if you're Mel Brooks. Mostly, though, forget it. And that which will bring one audience-member to tears of sadness will cause another to groan contemptuously. All we can do is try.

Those realities notwithstanding, we do have a *lot* of control. And, in choosing the all-important introductory moments, despite the virtual certainty that different audience members will react in varied, not *always* predictable ways upon meeting our characters, we writers must decide *how*, best-case, we would prefer those first encounters to go. How *much* we reveal, what we wish to hold back.

Now, as suggested above, you can *mislead* your audience. That's not merely acceptable — it is often to be desired as a dramatic tool, a storytelling device. But do it *intentionally. Plan* your later reveal(s) of who this girl or that guy *really* is, handled in ways that will surprise.

Restated, if *you* find it easy to introduce your characters, you're probably doing it wrong. By which I mean that you are not sufficiently challenging yourself.

The extra effort *will* pay off.

Examine the work of the superior novelists and screenwriters and playwrights. Notice how they decide to *show* us their characters. The precise first moment that the writer selects. The note that's struck.

There's an art to it. What follows is about the craft.

Exposition

Don't *tell* it.
Show it.

Another lesson from Screenwriting 101 that ports readily to *any* kind of fiction writing. As urged above, always *try* – when introducing your characters – to *show* them *doing* what they do. Engaged in their profession, craft, thing, whatever.

Yet another, even *more* compelling reason: verbally *telling* about an aspect of a character (profession, tic, quirk, attitude, etc.) will *not* stick to the audience's ribs. *Showing* the character *doing* it, *being* it, is what makes the lasting impression.

Now that's clearly not always going to be easy, possible, or even appropriate. For instance, simply in order to *show* your character being a lawyer, it would be a mistake to shoehorn into your story a scene in a lawyer's office, or in a courtroom. Obviously, there are other contexts in which an attorney can practice, and deeper into this chapter, you'll find several specific suggestions for getting around the problem. *But* – if such a scene *can* be inserted with grace, if it's organic to your story, it is definitely to be desired.

Amateur Exposition – The Dreaded "*But, you are my sister...*" Syndrome, and Other Sins

As suggested, in fiction writing there aren't a whole lot of *rules* that *cannot* be broken. But what you're about to read is one of my own (and is thus arguably a matter of personal taste), that for me comes about as close to inviolable as "The Rifle Above the Mantelpiece."

Do not *evereverever* communicate a character's occupation or background or relationship by having another character say anything remotely like "So, Al — how's the lawyering business?" or "...But, you *are* my sister..."

Ever.

You've seen worse? That's not an excuse.

Here's worse: *self*-exposition. As in "...but I *am* your brother..." Or having the above-cited lawyer *say* "As your lawyer, I..."

That is *bad* writing. Correction. It is *terrible* writing.

No, make that *beyond-awful* writing.

Do seasoned, even talented professionals write that way? Regrettably, carelessly, sometimes they do. Yes, we've all seen that sort of thing in work we might otherwise admire.

Just don't admire that part of it.

Or, put another way, how often — in what passes for real life — do you hear people say "...Back in '98, when we were at Stanford..." or "I'm your husband, and I..."?

Another way of stating it: *Desperately* avoid having your characters restate stuff they *both* already *know*, unless they're also adding something new.

Doing so is right up there on the no-no scale with telling your audience what *it* already knows.

Which raises the question of *how* to communicate that this one is a carpenter or a doctor or whatever, or that one is a sister. The answer should be part of your mindset. It isn't difficult. It's about avoiding the obvious.

For instance, "Mom said we should..." very nicely, and some-what obliquely, communicates siblinghood without beating it into the audience's consciousness.

Notice also that the possessive "Our mom" was unnecessary (unless the line was addressed to a non-relative). And, had it been used, it would have been bad writing.

Obvious is bad. Redundant is bad.

Oblique is good. Indirect is good.

A cautionary word about this last: while you're going for oblique and indirect, you have to guard against crossing the line – to unclear or obscure.

Good indirect/oblique might consist of having your attorney-character reply to a lunch-offer or other request for his time with

"...Okay, but we'll have to make it a quickie. I've gotta file this brief by 4:30..." *begins* to tell us what he does for a living. Or start the scene with your attorney on his celphone, instructing his assistant: "...And paragraph three sub-one-point-two should read 'lien-holder has the sole and unencumbered right to...' and so-forth..." And then, after he rings off, get him into the meat of *your* business. We now know A) what he does, B) that he's probably good at it, and C) he's decisive. And even a little about the type of client he's representing. *Not* an inconsiderable amount of detail to pass on to your audience with only a brief speech.

Are there *ever* times when *Obvious* or *Redundant* are desirable? Sure. As when they are essential aspects of a particular character. I'll address that further in the next chapter.

Front-loading — Some Advice — and Some Solutions

Don't front-load your exposition.

Sure, you've fully imagined your characters, given them complexity and dimension. You've created concise, solid biographies for them. You know a *lot* about them (though you'll learn more as your story progresses), and you're anxious to *use* it, to tell your readers about it.

Resist, with *all* of your strength, the temptation to squeeze all that great stuff into the first scene, into those first moments that this or that character is onstage.

Dole it out.

In TV we call the gradual reveal of a character – not terribly cleverly – *Peeling the Onion*.

Why is this important? For the same reasons cited at the beginning of this book. It's about *grabbing* the audience, your readers or viewers. You want them to keep on turning the pages. To *stay* with you, so they can learn how it turns out.

Similarly, to repeat, it's best to avoid a lot of plodding, *obviously* expository scenes at the top of your story. Television people describe this phenomenon, pejoratively, as *laying pipe*. We've all seen it, in everything from novels to movies to miniseries and onward. It's boring. Even to the least sophisticated, the least writing-hip audiences – people who may not know – or even care – *why* their attention is wandering – but will damned-well let *you* know by bailing out on your book, tuning out your show, or leaving the theater early.

Again, better to start in mid-story, to meet your characters at a crucial moment of an exciting – or at least intriguing – incident – and then lay that stuff in as you go. Often it's worthwhile to disorient your audience at the beginning – to make 'em wonder for a few minutes what or who in hell they're reading about, or seeing. *Use* the *gradual* revelation of character to *tease*, to *hook*, and then to *hang onto* your audience. To capture, to *entertain*.

FIVE

CONSTRUCTION – TELLING YOUR STORY

Plotting – Laying Out Your Story

Okay. You've started with the *idea*. The paragraph describing what your story is about. You've built it to a page, and now you're expanding it into an outline – either a detailed one, or simple steps. You've begun your character bios. You're becoming acquainted with your players. And you're laying in the classic three-act structure so that your story will *drive* toward those curtains.

For those who are unclear about what the traditional three acts consist of, here's the short-form:

Act One, put your protagonist up in a tree.

Act Two, throw stones at your protagonist.

Act Three, get your protagonist out of the tree.

Even if, as in *Romeo and Juliet*, the way out is death.

A theorist or two may have told you that the three-act structure is dead (likely it came from the above-referenced experts who are collectively twenty-eight cents short of being professional fiction writers). Don't listen to them. There are sound reasons for why it's worked for millennia, from folk tales to bible stories to Shakespeare to sitcoms, epic novels and miniseries. Among the more important reasons: it delivers *satisfaction*.

In TV we refer to the process of laying out our story, of planning the essential scenes, and sorting out the order in which they take place as *"breaking its back."* Not an inappropriate description, since it is often, especially on the more complex shows, a painful exercise. And, it can be time-consuming, sometimes taking several days. One of the ways it's done – a method that helps us maintain that so-necessary overview – is to divide a sheet from a legal pad into three sections – or, as described earlier, in one-hour TV drama, into four, because the commercial breaks every twelve minutes-or-so dictate that we write four acts – though in truth we're still using the traditional structure, simply adding another curtain-moment. Then, we fill in capsule descriptions of each scene. Often, as stated, we *begin* with our Act-Outs, or curtain scenes, and any other obligatory parts of the show's structure.

For action/adventure shows, these act-breaks are usually cliffhangers – moments when things look bad for the protagonist. A setback.

The same is true – in a less melodramatic sense – for the softer, quieter, more relationship-oriented shows. And for comedies, wherein the cliffhanger can/should be funny.

In cop or detective series, the Act-Out is often a shocker, an imminent crime, the discovery of a victim, or the reveal – or contradiction of – a key piece of evidence.

In *Murder, She Wrote*, where we usually kept the carnage down to a single homicide (we referred to the event itself as the "body-drop"), it mostly provided our Act One break, or at the latest, our mid-show (Act Two) curtain. And, as mentioned earlier, we could pretty well predict that our "penny-drop" would be at the end of *our* Act Three, or near the top of Four.

It's an approach that translates well to theatrical pieces, chapter endings for novels, even for childrens' books, sermons, non-fiction – even to poetry.

And of course, while the divided legal pad format is an effective way to work on shorter-forms, in a novel we're wrestling with a beast far more complex than a TV episode.

Back to your story structure, once you've completed your outline you should be able to *see* the whole of it with sufficient clarity to have a sense of your pacing, the dramatic and/or comedic highs and lows, the places that need tweaking, juicing-up, including spots where your story might be better-told if you changed the order of some scenes. Further, you should be able to judge how well your characters are fitting in, whether or not you're keeping them sufficiently "alive," where they need some help, and how well you're building to your pivotal story-points.

You'll also see where you'll need to add subplots (conflict) that will put *all* of your characters to work – another of the many good things that happen when you're writing your outline. And because in this relatively simplified form the holes in your story will be more visible, more readily spotted, they *should* be easier to plug, whether you fill them by inserting a plot device – or an additional motivation – or by shifting your characters around, by combining one with another. Or – creating a line of conflict between a couple of characters who seem to be "dangling," not carrying their weight (usually because there is no *edge* between them).

It's also where you'll be making discoveries about your characters, though in my experience, they usually don't begin seriously "talking to me" till I'm into the actual manuscript. But in the outline you'll be finding the drama/humor – adding those sparks of humanity – in even the smallest, mechanically-necessary scenes. You may realize that a path you've chosen for one of your players can take a detour – wander a little, thus making room for conflicts, attitudes and moments you hadn't anticipated.

The truth is, building your story in outline form is a difficult part of the process – the primary reason, I suspect, that so many writers resist it – but it's also a lot of fun. Or it *should* be. And for me – and my comfort-zone, it beats the hell out of the stress of *The Tightrope Act* – starting with "Fade In," "Once upon a time..." or the like, and trusting some sort of karma – or your characters – to guide you the rest of the way. That's how – unless you're gifted like the redoubtable Stephen King – one ends up with an unfinished "where does my story go now?" novel, or worse, one that meanders for 1000 pages and is unreadable and unpublishable.

The unfolding of your characters and their stories will of course be ongoing, continuing throughout the writing, but as stated earlier, repeated, and now restated once more:

> **Your outline is the part of the process at which the problems are easiest to see, easiest to fix without pulling threads, without that *awful* panic that strikes when, 250 pages into your novel or in the third act of your stage-or-screenplay, you realize that changes are *necessary*, but *they may cause your entire contrivance to unravel.***

And *never* delude yourself that your story – in order for it to hold an audience – is not *very much* a contrivance. In television I came to regard scripts as fragile constructs – houses of cards that, without careful shoring up, or with too much tinkering, can *easily* collapse.

Which, I believe, is part of the reason so many major movies are so deeply flawed; too many hands stirring the screenplays. The same can be true of novels. I know a number of writers who, while seeking representation, have been given conflicting editorial advice by agents who ask for this or that change in the manuscript before they will commit to handling the project. Sometimes their comments are constructive. Sometimes not.

It's important to *believe* in what you write – to *not* be looking to others for approval. Admittedly, that can be a difficult place to reach – particularly when you're new to writing. But it's a worthy, necessary goal.

Plot Conveniences, Holes, and
Other Audience Distractions

Going back to questioning your work while it's still in outline form, and then throughout the writing process itself, one of the key *hard* questions to ask is: does this or that scene or incident *move* your story? Is it advancing the plot? Is it taking your characters *and* your audience to a different place? If it's there solely because, for example, a character *must* receive a certain piece of information, or for you as the writer to plant some, as in *making* a certain event happen so that down the line something else can happen, if it's sole purpose is to platform something – if any of these are the scene's *only* reason for being, *that's* a *convenience*.

Fix it, or get rid of it. Rethink it.

Because *beyond* being bad writing, over and above the fact that your audience *will* pick up on it, *you should demand more of yourself.*

Okay, what *other* dimensions can you add in order to justify such a scene, to make it integral to your story? The advancement of a sub-plot is one way to go. Or introducing a new one wherein, say, a character suddenly finds he's got a fresh problem – with another player – or with something external.

Again, hard question: does the scene contain conflict? Are your character's goals, needs, attitudes and points-of-view part of that scene? Or is it just talk – in broadcasting it's called *fill* – speeches that do not need to be there, or could be spoken by anyone? Is it nothing more than a transaction in order to ease your continuity along to the next scene? Among the better TV series writing staffs such sloppiness is described contemptuously as "Television Writing."

Another tired contrivance that should be rejected is the *Withheld Information Gag*, or, as we also refer to it in TV, *The I Love Lucy Setup*. This classic piece of illogic was the basis for virtually every episode of that landmark series, *and* one of the reasons for its success – and I suggest that you *never* use it. Briefly stated, the formula went like this: if Lucy had only admitted, at the top of the show, that she had A) dented the fender of Ricky's car, or B) spent the rent money he'd entrusted to her, or C) forgotten to take care of some detail for which he was counting on her – or any of a hundred variations on the gag – there would be *no* story.

So, for the entire length of each episode, Lucy would do her damnedest to keep Ricky from learning the truth. Sometimes they flipped it, and Ricky would be the withholder, or it might be the Mertz's. That's all. It worked because we, the audience, bought the package, the fantasy: the ditzy, adorable redhead and her Cuban bandleader husband. We loved it – and them. We still do.

Obviously, *nobody* would try such a thing in a gritty, realistic novel.

And *certainly* never in the so-literal medium of big-budget, star-vehicle movies. Except that they did a few years back – and audiences, if they thought about it at all, are still scratching their heads, asking themselves the same nagging, dumb question that was on their minds through the *entire* film, while they *should* have been enjoying the show. The movie: the hugely successful *My Best Friend's Wedding* (Scr. Ron Bass – Dir. P.J. Hogan). The question: If the star, Julia Roberts didn't want Dermot Mulroney to marry Cameron Diaz, *why in hell didn't she just say so* at the beginning of the picture, instead of unaccountably – and *unbelievably* – keeping it to herself?

This otherwise well-played, well-made movie, with its talented, attractive stars, fell apart for me – and for many others – from the opening scenes onward – *because the question was in our minds* – and it was *never* resolved. Further, to communicate her objections to the union, and to break it up, the super-appealing Ms. Roberts was forced by the script to play a series of unattractive, mean-spirited tricks on the couple. Even Julia's legendary smile couldn't overcome the sour taste in our mouths, the result of her character's massively unfunny, psychotic, passive-aggressive behavior.

Sure the film made money. Sure, you probably enjoyed it on some qualified level. But we cannot know how much more successful the film might have been, how many more people might have put their friends onto it, if it had a storyline that made sense.

Again, I urge you *not* to construct a story on such a flimsy footing – *unless* you are fortunate enough to have Lucille Ball as your leading lady.

In a real way, the message for us as writers – both from the above, and from what follows – is to *respect* the audience.

Plugging Plot Holes

Often related to Plot Conveniences (or Contrivances) and every bit as damaging to a story, are Plot Holes. Illogic. Inconsistencies. Questions raised: Why didn't the bad guy simply do X? Why didn't the protagonist look in the closet in the first place?

Holes often tend to appear because the writer *wants* such-and-such to happen in the story, and logic is frequently the victim. Early in my writing career, I developed a kind of personal guideline that's worked well for me in such situations:

Play the *Reality*

Which means that when you're tempted to go into some sort of plot and/or character contortion in order for this or that complication to take place – the kind of contrivance that can come back and bite you on the ass – back off for a moment, and ask yourself what would normally happen in real life – what would the next step be, and maybe the one after?

It's almost a certainty that the complication you're trying to achieve can take place during that *believable*, non-audience-jarring course of events – that it can happen contortion-free. Consider the previous example, *My Best Friend's Wedding*. There are several ways by which the *I Love Lucy* gag could have been avoided, and the movie would have been better for them. One would have been for the Julia Roberts character to plead her case to Dermot Mulroney, and have him reject it, and her, for some false reason – such as believing that marrying the Cameron Diaz character is the only way for him to solve a certain problem in his life. Or, he's convinced – mistakenly or not – that the Julia Roberts character has in some way betrayed him. Or. Or. Or...

We've all experienced such distractions in novels, TV and movies. Sometimes, especially when the story is very compelling, we choose to overlook them. Sometimes not. And when it's 'not," when the hole *jumps* out at us, or even naggingly diverts our attention, the writer is losing the audience.

That's *fatal*.

Plugging plot holes is, like so much else in writing, about challenging yourself. Being on the lookout for such inconsistencies in your own material. The outline stage is where they're easiest to recognize, and easiest to fix.

And they *should* be fixed.

Interestingly enough, on all but the tackiest TV series, such holes are routinely fixed before the script is okayed for production. I suspect that the reason is simple: in TV, *writers* are in charge. Often, we refer to the fixes as "bolstering" a particular event or story-move. As mentioned earlier, in theatrical motion pictures, the director runs the show, which may account for much of the "careless" writing that plagues so many big-budget American films. Most directors are not writers. Another contributing factor is Hollywood's almost religious belief that the more writers they throw at a screenplay, the better it will become.

Wrong.

This was less of a problem during Hollywood's "Golden Age" (roughly 1930-1948), when the major studios were really more like today's TV networks. As suppliers of what was then the nation's number-one form of entertainment, they owned their chains of theaters (think: the TV sets in our homes), for which they had to grind out a steady stream of product (as with weekly TV series, etc.). In that era, when the population of the U.S. was about 130 million, there were weeks that topped 100 million admissions. Unlike today's movie production, there were heavy, autocratic (and usually, *talented*) hands on the controls – namely those of the moguls. Harry Cohn, Sam Goldwyn, Jack Warner, Darryl Zanuck, David O. Selznick,

L.B. Mayer and a few others. As is the practice in today's TV, most of them employed writers to oversee the scripts written by other writers. Moreover, directors, producers and actors rarely had anything approaching final say about the material.

While there are some very talented directors and producers making today's theatrical films, there are *many* more whose legendary disdain for writers and writing (read, in some cases: outright contempt) – as well as for the audience – may account for the current paucity of memorable movies, and the high incidence of those with plot holes and other basic, solvable script problems.

Did the Golden Age chiefs and their studios make bad films? Of *course*. They made a *lot* more turkeys than they did classics. But the legacy of good ones that are still a joy to watch all these years later at least *seem* to outnumber the more recent movies that are worth revisiting. But then, the same appears to be true of novels, TV, and of art in general.

Actually, however, I suspect that "good old days" thinking can be a trap, something of an illusion – that the ratio in *any* medium of good-art-to-bad-art is more-or-less constant. It's likely that at any given moment in history there are never a *lot* of great creative geniuses abroad in the land. Which is why we should be so thankful for the occasional Austen, Michelangelo, Dostoevsky, Fitzgerald, O'Hara, Puccini or Degas – the rare Chaplin, Sturges, Lelouch, Ingmar Bergman or Woody Allen...

How to Get Ahead of Your Audience – and Stay There

The plot hole is but *one* of the many ways a writer can lose the audience. Predictability is another. We've all experienced it – that feeling as you're reading a story, or watching a movie or TV show, that you *know* what's going to happen next. That the hero is about to be hit over the head, or the body is going to fall out of the closet, or isn't it about time for something bad, funny, stupid (or otherwise predictable) to happen?

And then, surprise, surprise, you're right.

As a reader or audience-member, when we're right, when we see it coming, we feel somewhat smug.

And disappointed. Which, for us, *and* for the writer, is *The Bad News.*

We don't *want* to be ahead of the story. And in our minds, it *forever* devalues the author's work.

The trick, then, is to set 'em up to expect a fastball, and then deliver your curve. What follows are several techniques I've absorbed from movies and TV that will help you stay ahead.

First, let's talk about joke-structure. There is a huge lesson to be learned about staying ahead of your audience – and *not* incidentally about basic, solid storytelling technique – from *the* classic form for comedic sight-gags. And remember, this applies to writing *anything*, comedy *or* drama, slapstick or suspense, satire or soap opera. The structure goes like this:

Man walking down the street, reading his newspaper.

Cut to the banana-peel in his path, setting up the audience to expect that he'll slip on it.

Back to the man: at the last second, he notices the banana-peel, sidesteps it – and falls into an open manhole (which neither he *nor* the audience has seen).

That's all there is to it.

But – consider all that it embodies.

It sets up the audiences' expectations, seemingly yanks the rug, and then delivers satisfaction. It is, in those three simple moves, the *essence* – not *only* of good physical – and verbal comedy – but again, also of good *storytelling.*

Substitute whatever you want for the man, his distraction, the banana-peel and the manhole. A young woman fearing a rockslide, who instead gets hit (or almost hit) by a car. A kid sneaking a cigarette – his mother's coming – it looks as if she'll catch him, except that she leaves the house. He breathes a sigh, home free – and inadvertently knocks her special dessert onto the floor, ruining it. Or breaks one of her prized chotchkies.

Now – consider how *un*satisfying it would have been if our anticipation was correct. If the man *had* slipped on the banana-peel. Sure, it's *sort of* funny, as is any classically executed slapstick pratfall. The audience will probably laugh.

But simultaneously, there will be disappointment – *because the viewers were ahead of the writer*.

The films of Chaplin, Harold Lloyd, the Marx Brothers, Laurel & Hardy, and more recently, Monty Python, Steve Martin, Eddie Murphy and Jim Carrey are for *any* writer well worth studying. For their timing, their great physical abilities, but most of all because their gags *work*, not only in terms of humor, but as well-told stories that – with their rarely predictable payoffs, keep them ahead of the audience.

But, in the vein of learning more from bad stuff than from good, I'll cite another example. Some years ago, film director/writer Blake Edwards made *The Pink Panther* (Scr. Blake Edwards, Maurice Richlin – Dir. Edwards). Wildly successful, it was followed by several sequels. While most audiences *loved* them, I found the films excruciatingly unfunny. The reason: Edwards paid off virtually *all* of his gags by showing the banana-peel, and then having the man slip on it.

There were *no* surprises. Except, initially, that he *went* for the obvious.

As with the probability that *I Love Lucy* would not have worked without the gifted Lucille Ball, I suspect that if Edwards hadn't cast the wonderful British comic actor, Peter Sellers, playing the bumbling hero, Inspector Clouseau, the series wouldn't have fared nearly as well. Those movies managed to be more-or-less amusing, *despite* the man who made them. But his non-Clouseau movies suffered doubly, from the heavy-handed joke-delivery *and* from the absence of Mr. Sellers.

A brief additional lesson from joke-structure that's worth noting, *especially* if you're writing comedy, is that a sequence of three (of almost *anything* – from put-downs to pratfalls to problems) is funny.

Two, however, is *not* funny. Nor are four in a row. But three *is* funny. I'm not sure why this is so, but it happens to be true.

And oddly – in terms of setup and payoff, the *principle of three* is every bit as valid for non-humor, for even the soberest, most dramatic stories. Two is usually not enough to make your point, and four will tend to be excessive.

Back to remaining ahead of your audience, in mysteries where, as mentioned earlier, you're essentially playing a game with your readers or viewers, it's an obvious, *suicidal* mistake to allow them to get ahead of you, to permit them to anticipate your moves and solve the puzzle before you and your detective character reveal its solution.

Every bit as bad, in mysteries or thrillers or procedurals, it's a *major* boo-boo to let audiences feel smarter than the *heavies*.

But worse yet – in *any* kind of story – is allowing them to feel smarter than the *author*.

How does one insure against this? There are several ways. One is to withhold, disguise or otherwise obscure, certain information, so that ideally it *only* becomes clear to them *when you want it to* – as when your protagonist puts it all together, or when you construct your story so that a certain event triggers such a solution.

Earlier, I alluded to the most startling and successful example of this that I have ever seen in print, executed by Richard Condon in his marvelous suspense novel, *The Manchurian Candidate*. Midway through the story, Condon lays in a small detail in which the unnamed, mysterious, key heavy sustains a minor hand injury. Then, for many pages, the incident remains meaningless (but stays with the reader), until deep into the Third Act when, by having one character casually ask the *least likely* character how her hand was injured, the reader suddenly learns the heavy's identity. It is a WOW! The revelation not only stunned me – it sent me riffling frantically backward through the book, searching out the account of the injury – I *needed* to make sure I hadn't misread it. It remains, for me, the most dazzling literary trick I've ever encountered.

I borrowed the device from Condon in writing *The Sixteenth Man*. Mine is a pale imitation, but *effective*.

Given the sophistication of today's audiences, the problem of staying ahead of them has become more of a challenge for writers of fiction than ever.

One way to view it is via the arithmetic: by the time the average American reaches the age of, say, 20, he or she has no doubt viewed *thousands* of hours of TV and movies. *Stories*. Many will have read dozens or even hundreds of novels.

They have *been* there – again and again.

All of the plots and devices and techniques.

Because of this saturated exposure – as with my own experience when I took up writing – *they* know a whole lot more about storytelling – both good and bad – than they may be able to articulate.

Which is one of the reasons that, 85 or 132 pages or so into the latest highly-touted bestseller, so many of us bail out. Or we punch *eject* minutes into the rented video or DVD, or walk out of movie theaters feeling dissatisfied (either vaguely or specifically), even after viewing an entire film we may have on several levels enjoyed.

The reasons for our disenchantment might be any (or several) of those mentioned above, or some you'll find further along in this book. Again, it's about *entertaining*. About *grabbing* – and then hanging onto your audience.

That's do-able, solvable, something that we can *learn* to handle. As writers, the important point is to be aware of our challenges. Passion alone is almost *never* enough.

Knowing What to Include – and What to Leave Out

As with reducing dialogue to its essentials, occasionally there are whole scenes we can leave out of our stories. What are some of the criteria? Is the scene *essential* – a step that the audience *must* witness? A description, say, of a character doing nothing more than exiting a room, moving down a corridor and into another room – which you may have written because it's easier than figuring out an alternative transition? Another yardstick: is it a moment that, if omitted, will leave your readers confused? Which, by the way, is not *always* a bad thing. It's the level and frequency that can cause problems. It is a long way from momentarily (for dramatic purposes) disorienting your audience – to baffling them about what you're trying to say, and having them wonder why they're bothering. Continuing with the criteria: is the scene or incident sufficiently interesting, entertaining enough to survive the cut? Does it add to or detract from the narrative pace, from the progress of your tale?

Sometimes, the omission of a particular scene can cause a subsequent moment to become *more* effective. An example: While I was Story Editor on yet another (mercifully) short-lived action-adventure show, I had turned in a script in which the show's teenage protagonist comes home with his pals, gives his mother a perfunctory hello as he and the others dash upstairs. The kids enter the young hero's bedroom/lair/hangout – and are startled to find the bad guy waiting for them, a dangerous convict whose prison escape they'd earlier, unknowingly abetted by playing a video game with him on the web.

I did *not* include the scene in which the convict entered the house and managed to enter the kid's room because as a storyteller I knew the sudden reveal I had written would *also* be startling for the viewers – superior in this case to setting them up to *anticipate* the kids' reactions. It was an easy choice for me – a no-brainer. And yet, when the show's Executive Producer finished reading my script, he asked me how the convict had gotten into the house in the first place. I looked at him in disbelief: "Who *cares*?" He told me that he did, that he wanted me to write that scene, include it in the script.

Now, this was *not* my first inkling – in the three-or-four weeks I'd been on the show – that as writers – or for that matter, as human beings – he and I were probably never going to find ourselves on the same page. But it *was* the one that tied it for me. With as much diplomacy as I could muster, I pointed out that the convict could have gotten there by several methods: He could have rung the doorbell and given the mother some kind of phony story – or he could have sneaked in without her knowledge – or broken into the house when nobody was home. I explained that after weighing those unentertaining, mundane, all-too-predictable options against the value of surprising both our hero and the audience (which, I figured, wouldn't have given a damn *how* the convict got in – anyway), I had chosen to write it the way I did. The Executive Producer, however, was adamant – he *wanted* that scene. I refused. I would *not* write it, would *not* waste screen time on such a scene, adding that if he wanted it badly enough he would have to write it himself – *and* in the bargain remove my name from the script (lest anyone might think I would write that badly). Further (and obviously at that point superfluously), I offered that things were clearly not working out for us, and that I was quitting the show.

When the episode finally aired, it was as I had written it.

Backstory

In simple, *backstory* is anything that your characters experienced, or that happened in your plot, before the first page of your tale. Mostly, it's important that *you*, the writer, know the backstory. But sometimes for clarity, context, dramatic purposes, or other reasons, it's necessary to *include* backstory in the piece you're writing. The danger is in *how* you write it. Because done badly it can slow or stop the momentum of your story. Or, it can confuse your audience.

In TV and film, backstory is something we try to minimize, or ideally, avoid – the use of flashbacks having fallen into largely-deserved disfavor – a stylistic gag that proved tedious and worse yet, sometimes made it difficult for audiences to follow. That's a good guideline for narrative writing as well.

All right. But the story *you're* writing *requires* some history. Below are several approaches for handling backstory.

A timeworn, somewhat dated, but nonetheless effective method is via a preferably brief prologue or foreword. Not necessarily the most artful tactic, it *can* do the job.

Another way is to gradually lay it in as exposition *after* you've put your present-day story in motion – employing narrative voice or by sprinkling it into your characters' dialogue. In the latter case, *sprinkling* is the important word. As with character-exposition, don't worry about being elliptical, even cryptic, as you drop in *hints* of your backstory. It's not necessary to put it *all* into a single speech. As long as it ultimately comes together for the reader.

In my own scriptwriting experience, on those occasions when I was stuck with backstory, where it was necessary to *show* past events, I tried to limit them to the visual (a car crash, a fire, theft or violent act), rather than play them as dialogue scenes. And usually I tried to place them, prologue-style, at the top of the show, often with a caption indicating the date or time the event was taking place. Not, as mentioned, a bad way to deal with the problem when writing prose.

Still another, rather extreme backstory device is the one described on page 108, used – but not invented by – Susan Isaacs in her novel, *Lily White*, which I emulated in *The Sixteenth Man* – wherein the entire narrative jumps back-and-forth in time through alternating chapters. *But* in both of *those* cases the backstory was every bit as important as the main story.

Usually, however – as with so much of good writing – backstory should be limited by the old *less-is-more* doctrine.

Playing Fair

When I started writing TV murder mysteries, one of the lessons I had to learn quickly was the carefully observed rule that we *must* give the viewers an honest chance to solve the crime. It meant that we *had* to include what was referred to as *The Play-Fair Clue*. An explanation follows, but again – the principle applies to all sorts of writing.

As in other mysteries, toward the end of a typical *Murder, She Wrote* episode, when Jessica Fletcher revealed the killer, she usually described how she had arrived at the solution. Such moments are generally known among writers as *Morris-the-Explainer Scenes*.

They often included flashbacks (though we tried to keep those to a minimum) that would illustrate something that Jessica *and* the audience had seen or heard which, when put together with other clues, led her to the truth.

Customarily, one of these was *The Play-Fair Clue.* That decisive bit of evidence which we hoped, when we did it right, would cause the viewers to hit themselves upside their heads for not having spotted it. A glance or gesture, a word, an anomaly. The telltale smudge of lipstick on a lapel – a distinctive shade worn *only* by the victim, or a grease-spot where none should have been. When we displayed the flashback, sure enough, there it was.

But, truth-be-told, we *were* rather devious about it: when we showed it the *first* time, it was visible or audible for only the *briefest* instant. *Just* long enough to later *prove* we'd played fair with the audience – just enough that if the viewers had been looking or listening really, really, *really* carefully, they would (should) have noticed, and figured out the solution. It was, as noted earlier, a game we played twenty-two times a year for twelve years. Our viewers were long-since hip to the fact that this-or-that was *probably* a clue – they were *trying* to get *ahead* of us, ahead of Jessica – so we'd try to throw in red-herrings – clue look-alikes that weren't really clues at all. Our challenge, beyond staying ahead of *them*, was *to keep on fooling them.*

What all this means to the non-mystery writer is *mislead 'em,* but *don't* cheat 'em. Don't suddenly spring stuff on your audience that you haven't platformed earlier – though it's okay if you've laid it in the *sneakiest* way.

Point-of-View

The outline stage is also where – if you haven't done so already – you begin choosing your point(s)-of-view. And deciding where to shift to another.

In series television, it's pretty simple. As stated, write to the money – the star. Don't turn away from him or her for very many scenes in a row. That can apply to novels as well. But if your novel is an ensemble piece with multiple stories and protagonists, point-of-view is, as in that type of TV series, mini-series, or full-length theatrical movie, a bit more complicated.

Again, the TV model: we refer to it as "servicing" your principal characters – or sometimes, your actors – giving them appropriate, adequate, meaty-enough screen-time. In multiple-thread shows wherein several stories are being told in (mostly) parallel action, the technique is one of jumping back-and-forth, getting out of one story (cutting away) at a dramatically arresting moment – and picking up another ongoing set of conflicts. From which, of course, you've omitted the dull parts.

All of which translates very directly to narrative fiction and, of course, to playwriting.

However, in straight narrative prose, point-of-view is even more complex, requires more attention. And while my take on the subject was not something I learned in TV, but rather when I turned to novel-writing, I'm including it here because of its relevance.

The subject of point-of-view in the novel has been covered very nicely by – among others – literary super-agent Albert Zuckerman, who posits in his informative book, *Writing the Blockbuster Novel*, that for a novel to succeed, it should be told from the points-of-view of no more than four characters – total. Fewer if possible. And, he suggests, the point-of-view should *never* shift *within* the same chapter. There are other caveats in his book, and while all may be valid, as with so many guidelines about art, there are numerous highly successful writers whose points-of-view tend to jump frequently, and it seems to work not only for them, but also for their readers. The prolific and popular Donald Westlake is an excellent example.

In writing *The Sixteenth Man*, I found much of Mr. Zuckerman's book extremely useful, much of his advice a worthwhile discipline. But not all of it.

The way I handle point-of-view in my own writing of third-person narrative fiction is that, in basic terms, over the course of a single chapter, I only allow myself into the head of one character at a time, only describe the inner feelings, or write the inner-monologue, of that character.

Conversely, if another character in the same scene is expressing anything non-verbally, I, the invisible narrator, prefer to describe it *only* in objective, external physical terms (*She placed her hands on her hips*), without commenting on the *meaning* of the gesture (as in *She impatiently placed her hands on her hips*). I try to allow my point-of-view character to make the comment on it, either internally, as in: *He wondered why she was becoming impatient* – or – *her impatience reminded him of...* Or, he remarks on it via internal monologue, or verbally. So that we're seeing as much as possible through *his* eyes.

Often, such things are judgment calls, but as a first-time novelist trying to maintain a consistent narrative voice, I found such criteria extremely helpful.

Again, as with so many aspects of the craft, the techniques and much of the mindset work across almost any form of fiction writing, from TV to novels to movies and short fiction: select the character(s) from whose point-of-view you're telling your story, and then stick to them. Don't jump around unless there's a purpose.

Now, obviously, if you're telling an epic tale, covering many years, you'll have no choice but to shift. And yet, even in such a case, it's usually best to limit your points-of-view to a select few.

Focus

All-over-the-place is a phrase used to describe a script or story outline that is not focused – one that jumps around to the point of becoming unclear as to *what* it is about. Not a great way to go.

Crime and Punishment and *Gone With the Wind* come to mind as definitive examples highly focused stories. Both Raskolnikov and Scarlett O'Hara are focal figures. *They* were whom the novels were *about*. Yes, there were many other characters, each with their problems and stories and subplots, but neither Dostoevsky nor Margaret Mitchell ever forgot where "the money" was.

Even if you're writing a "sprawling" epic, it's important to maintain focus on what you want the story to say.

Scene Structure

Scenes, like entire stories, should have a dynamic – a shape. Beginnings, middles, ends. They should build *to* something – to whatever it is you want the scene to *accomplish*.

And having accomplished it – you should *get the hell out*.

Obviously, it is sometimes *necessary* to write scenes that are very, very brief and don't have room for much construction. Frequent examples of this appear theatrical feature films – particularly in the more self-consciously stylish ones – where they do a lot of fast cutting.

Even if you're writing a novel or short story, it's often effective to manipulate your audience in that same cinematic way. Quick cuts. Building suspense, as in the movie version of *Jaws*, where Spielberg used all kinds of cinematic devices to nail us to the edge of our seats – from the ominous music to the shark's point-of-view, to not letting us *see* the shark until deep into the movie.

But as in much of television, in novel writing, in storytelling generally, it's a good idea to construct your longer scenes by having them begin on one emotional level and end on another. It's something you can almost diagram, like one of those above-the-line-below-the-line waveform graphs.

Say for instance that your scene starts off with your characters at the tops of their emotions, in mid-fight or mid-argument. Unless the moment is extremely brief – intended for instance as parallel action – to simply let the audience know the fight is in progress – you don't want it to play at that same level of heat all the way through the scene. Why? Because it's monotonous. Because it *goes* nowhere. The emotions should taper off, maybe heating up again before you're out of the scene. Bumps, enroute to a relatively placid ending. Or perhaps it starts out quietly, and escalates. That's shape, that's a dynamic.

In television drama, we try to limit a scene's length to three pages, maximum. Among the reasons for this are, again, pace, energy, keeping the audience's attention. But it's also a valuable limitation in that it forces the writer to *get to the point* of the scene.

Which is *not* to suggest that the scene needs to progress in a straight line, bang-on, to whatever it's about, without going anywhere else. Without a detour or two. Quite the opposite. One of the most valuable gags I've learned in screenwriting is:

Have more than one thing happen in a scene.

Interrupt the action or the dialogue, for instance, by bringing another character into the scene to deliver a new piece of information that will carry the story to its next place, perhaps introducing a clock, a new or stakes-raising conflict, a crisis of some sort. Or, it can be done with a phone call. Or just a diversion that upsets the rhythm of the moment, an annoying or distracting incident, for example. In a way this can be regarded as yet another device, one that has value for advancing your story, or heightening drama. And/or it can give your characters something *else* to which they can react. Yes, we're talking another thumb-rule that one should not be locked into, but try it. Ever notice, in a restaurant, how often a waiter or waitress happens to interrupt the diners' conversation – particularly one in which a punchline is about to be delivered? *Use* that. More than anything, it can liven-up one of those necessary-but-less-than-riveting scenes, lending it energy – perhaps triggering an emotional spike when the interrupted person reacts angrily.

And, as with your story as a whole, your individual scenes should, as often as possible have surprise endings. Unexpected bounces and/or moments that reverberate. Something, no matter how small, that the audience isn't *quite* prepared for.

Choreography

Choreographing your scenes is one more technique that ports very nicely and meaningfully from TV and screenwriting to any kind of storytelling. What it amounts to, as stated earlier, is "directing" your players, giving them *business*, *picturing* them – and *describing* them – in *motion*, delivering their dialogue with something more going on than their hands merely dangling at their sides. *Doing* something besides – or perhaps instead of – just talking. *Animating* what might otherwise be a somewhat uninteresting talk-scene. This last is addressed at greater length in the chapter on dialogue writing.

In writing film and TV one quickly learns that while it's easy – and often very desirable to continually move the action from setting to setting, when it comes to shooting the script, those frequent moves can cause serious problems. Changing locations – even from one room to another – takes time, which translates to money. New camera setups, relighting and remiking. And *major* moves, from interior to exterior, or to different, physically distant outdoor locations, can be even more time-consuming and labor-intensive, usually requiring trucks and busses. These last are known as Company Moves. They're very costly, and understandably viewed by the bean-counters with extreme unenthusiasm.

Hence, in writing our scripts we try to avoid frivolous moves, location changes that aren't essential to telling the story and – *always* the decisive factor – keeping the audience entertained. Writers of narrative can afford to be a *bit* more casual about changes of locale, but I feel that generally – even in prose, the old caveat about less being more still holds true. Don't write "Company Moves" unless you're making a point.

Conversely, in scriptwriting – especially with regard to hanging onto our audience, and because the name of the game is *moving pictures*, we try to avoid long, static shots and/or too many talking heads.

One of the ways screenwriters accomplish this is by writing specific movement into our scenes. By choreographing them. By including what we describe as "parentheticals" (stage directions, really, such as *crosses, grabs phone, enters, exits*, etc.).

Another way we lend movement and energy to what might otherwise be a relatively motionless dialogue exchange is to make it a walking-talking scene (in film, sometimes known as a tracking shot).

As a writer of prose, think about all the ancillary – interesting and *believable* – incident that can occur while your characters are walking along an office corridor, or on a public street. The people they encounter, the shops or doorways they might pass, the distractions-and-or pauses while one of them eyeballs an item in a store window, or an attractive young woman, or they wait for a traffic light to change. Stuff that can heighten the drama or comedy you're writing, energizing and bringing *life* to your material.

But, as with TV and screenwriting, the moves we write into our scenes, the business we give our actors – *must* be for a purpose that's *organic* to the story. For exposition – a move or gesture that *says* something about that character. Or to make a dramatic point, from a pratfall to a reveal. To advance the story in some way.

Perhaps the most important point is that moves – choreography – changes of setting – should *never* be arbitrary, contrived – say – to fulfill some structural or purely expository purpose the writer may have. That's awkward, forced choreography, and your audience will sense it.

One of the marks of bad writing – in prose *or* for the visual media – is inept choreography. Pointless, illogical or unnecessary moves. Again, there may be times when you write it that way to enhance your story, to throw a curve at your audience. But *know* that that is your point.

Another way to approach scene structure and choreography is to

THINK Picture/THINK Action/THINK Dialogue — A Screenwriter's Approach

Let's start by thinking about *dialogue*. You've done your homework, you've outlined. You have a pretty solid idea of where you're going with it. But suddenly you come to a necessary scene that stumps you. Though you may know *what* it's supposed to accomplish in terms of an A-to-B goal, you cannot quite visualize *how* you're going to get it there.

One of the more useful techniques I've developed for "finding" a scene, for getting into a scene which I either don't know *how* to start, or one in which the "meat" is eluding me, is by writing the participating characters' "sides" (their lines, the he-said-she-said) in their entirety, with little or no attention to action or picture. In a way, it can be thought of as allowing the characters to write the scene for you. I've even done it by ad-libbing into a tape recorder, playing all of the roles.

Rarely do I use *all* of what they say. Sometimes *none* of it survives the cut. But I've found it a great way to develop a scene that I'm unclear about — a scene that, because of its subject, or objective in terms of storytelling, and/or structure, *needs* to be there, but isn't automatically coming alive in my head. Often, the process will lead to business and/or a dynamic I hadn't anticipated – stuff that may add dimension to the scene.

Now, the *action* part. Once the dialogue begins to gel, and I've gotten it all down, the next step for me in this particular process is cutting. Which may begin with finding places where the spoken words can be augmented – or better, supplanted by action or business. Those looks or gestures or pauses during which a character can take a sip of coffee – in place of a verbal response.

Or *even* better yet, finding material that can be *eliminated*.

And of course the *outside* trims – snipping off the *ends*.

At the the top, discovering how *much* I can can get rid of – how *deep* into the scene I can be when it begins. This part usually surprises – not only about how little is really necessary to make a significant story point, but also how *effective* it can be to throw your audience momentarily off-balance. Disorienting readers or viewers, wondering what in hell you're up to is, incidentally, another convincing argument in favor of peeling back your exposition a layer at a time.

And similarly, best-case, leaving them with their mouths agape at the far end of the scene.

And – the *picture*: Regarding descriptive passages, my

suggestion is that unless your name is F. Scott Fitzgerald and/or you have more than a touch of the poet, keep yours brief. Now, admittedly this may be a matter of taste, but in narrative fiction I find long paragraphs of scene-setting, of "eloquent" landscape description, and accounts of what people look like or what they're wearing, tedious. For one thing, they're usually not written very artfully. Also, such passages can stop the narrative flow. And, even when they're written beautifully, I confess that I often find them to be self-consciously literary. Moreover – and again, it's taste – I'd rather visualize the characters and the settings without a lot of help from the writer. Brevity, such as "Fortyish, with a whiskey-baritone" works far better for me than such details-upon-details as aquiline nose, silky skin-tone, gray-green eyes and more — unless of course they're truly *essential* to the picture the writer is painting.

Sure, sometimes elaborately delineated physical characteristics, or the finer points of how a room is furnished have their place. Principally, of course, if you're writing period stories, or scenes in which research is key. Even there, however, I recommend economy. Say it in as few words as possible. As in TV writing, let your action and dialogue carry the scene. Almost invariably, less *will* turn out to be more.

Stoppers

A Stopper is *anything* – from a clumsy or unclear piece of choreography, to awkward narrative verbiage, to a line – or single word – of dialogue that confuses – that *stops* the audience. One that causes a viewer or reader to wonder what was just said, or *why* it was said in that way. Sometimes it's the result of pretentious or self-conscious writing. Or a lack of clarity.

In narrative fiction, a Stopper interrupts the reader's flow. Admittedly, the need to re-examine – and pause to think about an occasional passage – probably won't cause the average reader to disgustedly hurl your book across the room. But it's a step in that direction, a move toward alienating your audience. And if you do so repeatedly it can be *very* harmful, even hurting sales of your next effort.

In theatrical pieces, film or TV, you can *really* lose your audience: If 200 – or 2,000 – or 20 million people are sitting there confused by what they've heard – or seen – you can be sure that many will lose the thread of the next few transactions – and in the bargain develop an intense dislike for the writer.

Another Stopper that should be avoided is the kind that inadvertently calls attention to, and comments on, the material itself. Deep into one of my early comedy scripts, following a series of funny pratfall-type accidents, I placed the following reactive line of dialogue in the mouth of the character who was most negatively affected by them: "Ogod, will this *never* end?"

Not a terrific idea to plant in your audience's mind.

Can a Stopper ever be desirable? Absolutely. As it was so beautifully executed by Richard Condon in *The Manchurian Candidate*. But for most of us, the safest, most effective place for them is at the end of a scene or chapter, or of an entire story – as a punchline. Something for the reader or viewer to reflect upon.

More About Where to Start a Scene and Where to End it
or
Why the Playwright's Curse is the Novelist's and Screenwriter's Blessing

Unlike the printed page or the movie-or-TV screen – either of which can provide close-ups or their equivalent, the theater stage is essentially, in movie-jargon, a wide shot. While adept stagecraft, and/or artful, modern lighting can isolate – and focus an audience's attention – on a particular part of the scene – even approximating movie-type cutting – the fact remains that it's still taking place at a distance from the viewer.

Another aspect of the Playwright's Curse – mostly the playwright is stuck with that tedious physical, logistical problem – the inescapable *need* to write entrances and exits – the *necessity* of moving actors on and off the stage. *And* with it, the challenge of keeping it entertaining.

Entrance Lines. From "Hello," to "Tennis, anyone?" – it's hard to come up with one that's fresh. Same with Exit Lines. Sure, there are some memorable ones, lines *that make a point*, that have impact because they are delivered on an exit. Largely, though, they are the bane of most playwrights' existence.

The screenwriter or novelist, on the other hand, can *start* in the *middle* of the scene!

And *should!*

Unless there's a helluvva good reason to open it at the beginning, by bringing a new person through a doorway and into a room, or onto a location, *don't*.

William Goldman's motto for this says it very succinctly: *Get into a scene as late as possible*. (The same can be said of your story as a whole.)

And – your scenes *can* be buttoned without anyone needing to leave.

Bringing a new person onstage – or having one exit, say, in anger – in the *middle* of an ongoing scene – *that's* something else, a device that can be very effective in introducing a new element – another level of excitement, conflict or humor.

Sure, there will be times when *seeing* somebody entering or exiting at the top – or bottom – of a scene is valuable, even essential. Obviously, a character bursting through a door on some sort of urgent mission (or storming out) can be highly effective (arguably, falling through a skylight is even better). But if the entrance you're imagining *isn't* dramatic, if it's just a ho-hum way to start, you don't *have* to write it that way. If the moment doesn't *count* for something such as character development or exposition, if it isn't adding anything – such as surprise – or urgency – or a button – or unless it has comedic value (as in Kramer's entrances and exits on *Seinfeld*), why do it at all?

One of my reasons for emphasizing this is that so many writers – even professionals – as they're devising a scene, tend to envision the entire transaction from the *beginning* – the client walking into the lawyer's office, for example, including the "Hello, how are you" business that usually has no dramatic/entertainment value whatever – and is at best mostly on-the-nose exposition. Alas, far too many otherwise competent novelists seem to think that because they've pictured that their hero has to enter a room and meet someone – even if the meeting has no dramatic weight – they feel obligated to include the non-event anyway. And they may imagine – and write it clear through to the excruciatingly dull end, when the characters say their goodbyes and so on, and then exit the room.

Don't.

As with dialoguing, imagining it's entirety is an okay approach to *creating* your scene – but *not* if you then leave it that way, without trimming the fat.

Far better, as indicated earlier, to take a hard look at the content and, by trimming both ends – and perhaps taking some nips out of the middle – end up with only the *good stuff.*

This includes finding, if you aren't already certain of it, the button for your scene – the precise moment at which you should end it, instead of hanging around after it's over and stepping on your punchline – diminishing its impact.

Punchlines, Buttons and Act-Outs

Scene-endings, curtain-lines, are challenges all of us face, though the playwright's may differ from those of the novelist or screenwriter, who can limit what the reader or viewer sees or hears – as much or as little as the author chooses. The equivalent, in film, of calling for a close-up, of focusing audience-attention where *we* want it.

I've already explained that the Act-Out (commercial-break) in television scripts carries with it an additional requirement, beyond that of a punchline or button in other media, to motivate the viewers – even if they channel-surf during the commercials – to return for the next part of the show.

Okay, but how does this apply to other writing-forms?

As a cautionary note. Make sure *all* of your scene-and/or-chapter-buttons are as *strong* as you can make them – especially if, in the next scene you're abruptly changing locales, dealing for example with parallel action.

Leave your audiences *hanging*. Make 'em *anxious* about what's going to become of the characters they've just left.

This caveat, by the way, is *not* limited to melodrama or suspense yarns. It *should* be part of the writer's thinking for even the softest, most lyrical of stories. It's another *essential* part of hanging onto your audience.

Often, the scene-button, the "out," is *not* a line of dialogue, but rather a moment, as in a look, a silent reaction from one of the players. Obviously, this is a lot easier for the writer to control in a novel, or in movie and TV scripts, than it is in a stageplay. And it is definitely a place where – in TV anyway – the writer can and should direct the scene *on the page*, with a specific instruction for actor, director and film editor:

"Off Millie's look, we go to:" Followed by the next scene.

Or:

"Richard sags."

Clearly, such cinematic stage directions would be unsuitable for all but the quirkiest novels. But *paraphrased equivalents* – written in the appropriate tense, in an acceptable prose style (in *your* style) – can be *very* effective in narrative fiction. And by limiting it to the outward description, rather than explaining the character's inner feelings, one can leave the audience, whether readers *or* viewers, with the opportunity to project, to *imagine* what is going on behind the character's eyes.

Nor is it wrong to button a scene from *inside* the mind of one of your characters.

A good button is a good button.

The *Non-Scene* – Causes and Cures

The scene in which all of the characters are in agreement with each other.

The scene inserted solely for the purpose of exposition, of passing along information to the audience.

The scene that is basically "mechanical" in the sense that its excuse for being there – its purpose – is to establish a certain fact, or to get this or that character from Point *A* to Point *B* for plot purposes.

The scene that merely platforms a story-element or clue without achieving anything else. Without adding anything new, or advancing inter-character conflicts.

The scene containing no dramatic or comedic value.

The scene that fails to *entertain*.

All of these are what we describe in television as *non-scenes*. And I mark them as such in scripts that I'm editing. They're dull, amateurish, and *not* acceptable.

They also have something else in common: If whatever they accomplish is essential to your story, they can almost *always* be incorporated into other, more interesting scenes.

It's worth repeating here that among the most important of the many self-editing questions you need to ask yourself is – *where is the heat in each scene*? Where's the tension in each moment? Where is the conflict? Where's the edge? What's going *on* in this transaction – *beyond* the transaction itself? Again, the heat need not be in *what* they're talking about or otherwise acting out, but rather in the *subtext*, a topic discussed more fully in Chapter Six.

Further, each scene should pass the writer's "What does it accomplish?" test. Does it move the story to another place? Does it expose another side of one or more of the characters?

If the answer is no, it's telling you to rethink it.

Non-scenes are what cause your audience to dial out. The good news is – the condition is *fixable*. In ways suggested earlier in this book, as well as others you'll figure out for yourself. Sometimes the solution will be to eliminate the scene, or to combine it with another. Or – to find another layer, another level further beneath the surface of one or more of your characters – one that provides the needed spark that will bring the scene to life.

But first, you need to *recognize* when you've committed a non-scene, to set your own detector to begin flashing when the problem shows up.

The toughest scene to write so that it won't be a non-scene is, as mentioned earlier, the love scene. The scene between two people who agree with each other. Because on the face of it, it doesn't have conflict, ergo it has no drama. Ergo it has no entertainment value. Even if it's gussied up with literal eroticism, or with jokes – unless the humor – or the acrobatics, contain *some* conflict.

Examine the earlier-referenced opening of Preston Sturges' film, *Christmas in July*, and you'll see one of the very best examples of how to make such a moment work. I think you will also be impressed by how much, in terms of subtle exposition, Sturges shows us about the couple – and how quickly he sketches it in – without being on-the-nose.

What continues to astonish me, in novels, television shows, and in so many big-or-small budget movies, is how often edges are missing from scenes, or even from entire stories. One of the liberating benefits of the VCR and DVD is that if a movie viewed at home fails to grab us in – say – the first fifteen or twenty minutes, we can – and do – bail out with less hesitation than if we'd laid out nine or ten dollars per theater ticket - plus overpriced candy and popcorn. Or popped for a pricey, over-hyped hardcover book that turns out to be unreadable.

Obviously, considering the number of such novels that are published, and films released, containing long, uninteresting, non-confrontational scenes, there are quite a few successful professionals out there who seem to disagree with me about the need for consistent, ever-present conflict as *the* tool for grabbing – and then holding onto – the audience. Are they wrong? I believe they are. Would their work be more effective, more involving, if they *did* agree? I *know* it would.

Or – could it *be* – they simply don't know any better…?

Next time you encounter a piece that fails to engage you because it lacks edge, or story, or compelling characters, I suggest that you question it in at least the following terms: *How* could the author have made it better? How, if you were given the opportunity of rewriting or editing the material, could *you* have made it better?

It seems a near-universal truth that it's far easier to learn from bad stuff than from good. The good – novels, short stories, plays, movies – seem to transport us into their world, taking us along on their ride, anesthetizing most of our critical faculties. At least until we revisit them.

And than there are those rare jewels – the *really* good ones – that get better as, with each encounter, *we* bring something new to the table. In my own experience, re-reading Scott Fitzgerald's *The Great Gatsby* at ten or fifteen-year intervals has been like reading a fresh, ever-better book each time.

The good ones *accomplish* what we, as writers, *hope* to do.

Kicking It Off – That *Super*-Critical Opening Moment

Where and how to *start* one's yarn – choosing the *just* right opening words for a novel, play or short story – selecting that *optimum* moment for the beginning of a screenplay or teleplay – the *crucially* important first meeting between your fictional creation and your audience is – once again – about *hooking* them.

Right up there in importance with how you choose to introduce your characters, those initial words involve creative decisions not to be taken lightly. Nor usually are they easily arrived at. The estimable novelist/screenwriter Elmore Leonard, by the way, suggests that most of us should *never* start with weather.

Look at some incredibly memorable opening lines, two of them dialogue, the others narrative:

"Now is the winter of our discontent…"
(William Shakespeare – *Richard III*)

Let me tell you about the very rich – they are
different from you and me…
(F. Scott Fitzgerald – *The Rich Boy*)

"Call me Ishmael…"
(Herman Melville – *Moby Dick*)

As Gregor Samsa awoke one morning from uneasy
dreams, he found himself transformed in his bed
into a gigantic insect…
(Franz Kafka – *The Metamorphosis*)

Or check out some great opening movie scenes, from *Raiders of the Lost Ark* (Scr. Lawrence Kasdan, Story by George Lucas and Philip Kaufman – Dir. Steven Spielberg), to *His Girl Friday* and others. Or the awesome first few minutes of *Butch Cassidy and the Sundance Kid* (Scr. William Goldman – Dir. George Roy Hill). Or *The Godfather* (Scr. Mario Puzo & Francis Ford Coppola, based on Puzo's novel – Dir. Francis Ford Coppola), in which a dozen-or-so characters are introduced, all of them – *and* their complex relationships – vividly-and-economically defined, riveting our curiosity. Examine how these films hook us, how deftly they handle exposition, how quickly they are *into* the story. Writers of *any* type of fiction, as well as authors of nonfiction, can learn a *lot* from the choices made, from the way those movies begin.

There is *much* about storytelling technique to be learned from the visual media, all the way from TV commercial spots to epic movies and miniseries. How it *looks*, and how it's *written*. The effective juxtaposition of sounds and images.

Has the influence of film and TV on narrative writing been consistently positive? Of course not. But cinema has *definitely* changed – and refreshed – the way novelists, historians and biographers practice their art.

I don't know that there is a for-certain technique for writing terrific opening scenes, nor any guarantee that yours will be as effective as those cited. But, like so much of the mindset I acquired while writing for TV, *awareness* of the problem – of the *need* for *truly* arresting hooks and grabbers – will ultimately improve your writing. And in any case, I deeply believe that what*ever* extra effort you put into such details will be rewarded – bigtime.

Payoffs and Blowoffs – The Endgame
or
More Fastballs and Curves

Endings.

Guy gets the girl. The murder is solved. Girl gets other guy. The world is rescued from the bad guy. Girl loses guy. The farm is saved. Justice prevails. Earthlings survive attack from outer space. Problems are cleaned up – or not. Loose ends are knotted, snipped – or not.

An ending is – an ending. But...

But – like a lot of the stuff of good storytelling, it's not that easy to do it well, to pull it off so that your audience says a collective "Wow!" The zinger, the twist, the topper they didn't *quite* expect. You know the kind – those *delicious* finishes you've encountered in *your* favorite novels, stories, movies. As with memorable openings, satisfying, drop-dead endings can be elusive, difficult to create.

But they're worth the striving.

In the action genre, whether TV, movies or novels, the end scene is often – and appropriately – described as the *blowoff*. A good way – for the writer's head – to regard the finish of even the most benign type of story.

How many times have we read novels where the last three or four pages were coda, where the whole thing just wound itself down, rather than presenting anything new – anything unanticipated? Satisfying, maybe. Blah, more likely. Like certain symphonic pieces that seem to end, but no, there's more – and then more. And movies? A notable example was a rather pleasant Bette Midler vehicle,

Beaches, (Scr. Mary Agnes Donoghue, from Iris Rainer Dart's novel – Dir. Garry Marshall) which seemed to have three or four endings. They'd play a "final" scene, at the conclusion of which the audience expected to see the end-credits. Instead, another scene was played, and then another.

Looked at another way, I suppose it can be argued that they were giving us their own brand of surprise, but I'm not sure that that was the filmmakers' intent.

Again using action films as a model, think of it as the challenge of coming up with a blowoff that *tops* all of the movie's earlier fireworks and razzle-dazzle sequences. A superb example of a film that accomplished this at the end of an already breathless, seamless, relentlessly paced story that was full of Big Moments (including the all-but-impossible-to-surpass railroad locomotive/prison bus collision), the finale of *The Fugitive* manages to leave the viewer exhausted and gratified.

But helicopters, explosions and shootouts atop tall buildings aren't a *requirement*. A much quieter though no less satisfying finish occurs in one of the best films ever made – the great, enduring *Casablanca*. Rick and Ilsa's final goodbye was – and still is – flawless, almost unsurpassable, speaking to all but the most cynical among us, about sacrifice and lost love. But the film *couldn't* end there. We *had* to see the plane taking off for Lisbon, as well as resolving Rick's having shot the German Officer, Major Strasser. And ironically, the final, unforgettable line of dialogue – *"Louie, I think this is the beginning of a beautiful friendship."* – wasn't even in the script. It was tacked on during the editing process.

Now – going for this type of ending seems on the face of it to be an obvious goal. And of course, from page one, you've been trying to give them stuff they don't expect.

But the *most important* one you're going to write is the one that *resonates* after the reader finishes your book, or your viewer turns off the TV or exits the theater. Sometimes it's big without being slam-bang – a moral, a comment about life, or the world. Often it's something small – smaller perhaps than the goal just achieved by your protagonist. A feelgood moment – or one that's eerily ironic. Or humorous. Or full of portent. Again, the key is that it should seem *unexpected* – yet satisfyingly *inevitable*. It should feel *right*.

Always, when you devise *your* endings, your story's final moments, your curtain-line – try to *surprise*. I'm not talking off-the-wall, come-from-nowhere, nonsense endings. I mean an end-frame that's legitimate, *organic* to your story, that comes from deep within your construct, or your characters – one that seems *right* – and causes the audience to – if not gasp – perhaps think about.

A Curtain that stays with us.

One of my favorites is the final moment, the last line of dialogue in *Three Days of the Condor*. Aside from its superb execution, it struck a chilling note back in 1972. Seen today, in the context of what we now know, it's spookily prophetic.

A few other killer endings: Steinbeck's *The Grapes of Wrath*, and John O'Hara's novella, *Natica Jackson*. Both will remain with you for a long time. As will the final, devastating shot in the wonderful, funny/painful film, *The Heartbreak Kid* (Scr. Neil Simon, based on a story by Bruce Jay Friedman – Dir. Elaine May). There are of course many others, and you probably have some favorites of your own.

Study them. Figure out what makes them work.

And then *steal* from them.

Admittedly, by the time we've completed our outline we may not always have found that stick-to-the-ribs, unexpected ending – the superbly orchestrated blowoff. Oh, we *should* be more-or-less there, have an *idea* of how it's going to end, but – things occur to us as we write – it's part of the process – and when it's *working*, when we *let art happen*, one of the fun parts.

But *certainly* by the time you reach the end of your story there should be that turn, that switchback (or maybe several) that maybe even *you* – weren't anticipating. I didn't find the closing lines for *The Sixteenth Man* until *after* I had finished what I assumed was my final draft. As with so many of the discoveries we make while in process, that one hit at about 4:30 AM, when it surprised the hell out of me, jolting me out of heavy sleep.

Which brings us to what is arguably the *most* important element in telling your story *and* in the portrayal of your characters, the one that goes beyond how they look, or move — the one that — if done well — will define them over and over for your audience: how they *sound* — how they speak. The *words* you put in their mouths.

SIX

WRITING GREAT, *UNIQUE* DIALOGUE

"*Unique* Dialogue" Defined

In the area of dialogue writing, I have a few heroes. Novelists Dashiell Hammett, Elmore Leonard and John O'Hara, playwrights Lillian Hellman, Harold Pinter and Clifford Odets, screenwriters Joe Mankiewicz, Bill Goldman (also a first-rate novelist), Callie Khouri, Anita Loos, Budd Schulberg, Dorothy Parker and Robert Towne. I do not include William Shakespeare because to me, having virtually invented the English Language as we know it, he occupies a realm of his own. I know that if I live four lifetimes I'll never be in the same league with those people, much of whose dialogue I would *kill* to have written. But it's a standard I try hard to achieve. To go for dialogue that — in every word or sentence uttered — *delineates* that character — could *only* be spoken by *that* character.

And yet – is *unexpected*.

Now, that's a tough assignment — but you might be surprised by how do-able it is. Maybe not with the brilliance of the above-mentioned writers, but – *respectably*.

Again, it's partly mindset. *Deciding* that that is how you're going to write.

The next paragraph is, for me, among the top two or three

things I've learned in writing scripts for film, TV and theater, all of which are of course *mostly* dialogue. It may be the single most important lesson you'll find in this book:

> ***If you can assign a block of already-written dialogue to another character without rewriting the dialogue, <u>you are doing it wrong</u>.***

It almost deserves to be a chapter all by itself. Read it again.

> ***If you can assign a block of already-written dialogue to another character without rewriting the dialogue, <u>you are doing it wrong</u>.***

Even if the content of the speech is nothing more than "Hello, how are you?" Or even just "Hello."

No two characters that you create — *if* you are doing your job, which means *if* you are *listening* to them — should express the same thought the same way.

Ideally, *every* line that a character speaks should be a *Character Line* — that is, it should help *define* that character, be *unique* to that character. Ideally. Each word we put in the mouth of a character — the way *that* character speaks – should be — distinctly, the singular way the character filters the world he or she occupies – the world *we've* created — as well as *where* the individual is coming from at that moment in our story. As *only* that character would say it.

I hasten to re-emphasize that I do *not* mean dialogue should be *self*-explaining, *self*-expository. As stated earlier, that is a *major* no-no.

Self-Explainers (and Other Works of Fiction)

Characters who can clearly, lucidly explain themselves – explain *why* they're doing this or that – should be at most a rare exception. As when your bad guy is doing his aria, telling us – as in the earlier-referenced *James Bond* movies, how and why he is going to rule the world.

Is it *ever* appropriate for them to explain themselves – say – obliquely? Sometimes. One of the very best – one that I wish I had written – is the monologue – almost a soliloquy – delivered toward the end of *Three Days of the Condor* by Joubert, the enigmatic assassin (marvelously played by Max von Sydow), in which he quietly, guilt-lessly expounds on the pleasures of his chosen profession. He might have been describing a career as a floral designer, or an academic. I've used that speech as a model in several of my scripts.

But self-deluding, or unable to see themselves as others view them — that's even better than articulated self-knowledge.

Outright lying to themselves — that's often as good as it gets. Why? Once again, because your audience will *connect*. Because of the character's universality. Because it's what most of *us* do.

Moreover, fictional characters who can tell us all about them-selves are *not well written*. How many people do *you* know who're *really* able to explain who they are? Elderly people, sometimes (though in real life I suspect the age/wisdom equation is overrated). Younger ones, almost never.

As emphasized in the section titled *Liars Play Better Than Saints* (page 89), and re-emphasized here, most of *us* are doing this-or-that number on ourselves *most* of the time. We're withholding things, or telling partial or outright lies to ourselves and to others. It's how we get through life.

And — unless you're writing about monsters, "we," albeit arguably in heightened form, are whom your characters should reflect.

Again, this is an important point because we can all *identify* with such traits. It is those quirks, those human frailties that make your characters *believable*.

But there's an even more compelling reason for not having your characters *really* understand themselves: accurate self-knowl-edge is generally *not entertaining*.

Rephrased, I don't know about you, but when I'm presented with a character who can – and does – explain him-or-herself, or who seems to *truly* understand what motivates him, I tend to not *believe* that character. Ergo, I zone out.

Okay – but suppose your story *requires* that some of that character-appraisal stuff be said, not by your novel's narrator, but rather, in dialogue. As stated before, one way to achieve this is by giving those personal insights, those pithy observations, to *another* character.

Why is that more believable? Think about people you know. Think about yourself. Most of us seem to have the answers to our friends' problems and/or shortcomings, yet very few of us can solve our own. Nor, I suspect, are most of us consciously aware of them, though they may be obvious to others.

Before moving on to other techniques of dialogue-writing, I want to impart another of my personal no-no's.

Never, *never* have one of your characters say, "What th'...?" *Not <u>ever</u>.*

Unless you're writing satire.

In *any* other context, it makes a statement about you – as a writer – as an ostensibly creative person – that you really will *not* want said. If I encounter "What th'...?" in a manuscript submitted by a writer looking to me for work – I read no further. Why? Because nobody outside of comic books ever says it. Because, worse than a cliché, it is the almost quintessential example of *mindless* writing – a nearly sure-fire indicator that there will be more of the same elsewhere in the material. That too much of it will be beyond fixing.

Once you've gotten past that first, get-it-all-down-draft (if that's your M.O.), mindless writing has no place in your work.

There is *no* mindlessness in good writing.

Hearing Your Characters' Music

In the early days of TV there was a hit sitcom called *My Favorite Martian* (Cr. Jack Chertok). Ray Walston, a veteran character actor with a wonderful, Broadway-trained sense of comic timing, played the Martian. Scanning the script for an upcoming episode, Ray was stopped by a particular line of dialogue written for him, and announced — perfectly seriously — "A Martian wouldn't say that."

When you're really cooking, your own characters will say things like that to *you*. *Listen* to *how they sound*. The tempo. Their individual rhythms. You'll know when you get to that place. And it can take awhile. You may not hit it the first time out — but don't give up on it.

And while you're listening, hear the *silences*. Non-verbal responses to the last line spoken. *Think* about how much can be said with a look, a gesture, a shift in body position. Whether you're writing dialogue for film, stage, or narrative, say as *much* as you can with *silences*. See *Listen to the Silences*, on the following page, and *Dialogue Attribution in Prose* (page 189) for some further thoughts on the uses of silence.

Subtext

Simply put, when employed in dialogue, subtext is people talking about things that have meaning on more than one level. Like most of us do in real life. A lot.

Viewing this from a slightly different angle, one of the most telling, most *cuttingly* precise critiques of another writer's work that I have ever heard was delivered by a fellow writer/producer as his reason for *not* hiring a particular freelancer: "All of his characters say exactly what's on their minds."

There is a genuine, resonant lesson in that comment, one that I keep near the top of my self-editing list. And significantly, the writer about whom it was said had a *very* abbreviated career. The rest of his stuff – from story-structure to scene description – was as *on-the-nose* as the dialogue he wrote.

Which is another way of describing an absence of *subtext*. In an essential way, subtext is the opposite of *on-the-nose*. And while sometimes, of course, subtext will be communicated by a character's actions, here we're addressing the phenomenon as it applies to dialogue.

The most legitimate uses of subtext in writing dialogue are, as in real life, in situations and/or places in a relationship where the individuals involved feel uneasy about confronting a subject directly. Where instead they talk around it. Sometimes by employing metaphors.

Can subtext be overused? Sure. As when writers get *too* cute — too indirect or symbolic, causing the audience to become confused about the author's point. But properly handled — and admittedly, like most art, the choice is part inspiration/instinct, part judgment call — such veiled exchanges can often be *far* more effective — and believable. Even more importantly, it *is* more *entertaining*, more intriguing than on-the-nose dialogue.

Functional Dialogue – and How to Avoid It

It's been my observation that many inexperienced writers create dialogue that I call *utilitarian* (another word for on-the-nose) — they write words that convey the *surface*-meaning — contain the basic information — of what they want the character to say, and then they leave it at that.

The result is flat, boring, uninteresting nuts-and-bolts dialogue. *Functional* dialogue.

Writers who have a knack for dialogue — and some experience — may also *start* with utilitarian first-draft speeches, *but then they rewrite them*, make them fascinating, vernacular, idiomatic, colorful, tantalizing, elliptical and/or inarticulate! Make them *Character Lines.*

Suggestion: next time you write dialogue, examine it from that point-of-view. Once the words contain the essence of what you want the character to say, read it aloud so that you hear how stilted and obvious it is. Afterwards, rework it so that it *sounds* like real speech. Then try reading it aloud again.

Listen to the *Silences*

While it isn't an essential part of the curve of learning to write effective dialogue, working with actors has for me been a revelation. Hearing and seeing them read lines I've written – observing which ones work, which don't, and best of all, which – because of an actor's skill – come out better than they were on the script page, is an experience I wish all writers could have. And one of the most vital lessons I've taken from that medium is how the *really* good actors employ *silence* when delivering their lines.

For me, silences are perhaps the most important — and most overlooked — aspect of good dialogue-writing. When one character *responds* to the words (or actions) of another with a hesitation before speaking — or frequently even *more* telling — without saying *anything*.

Sure, *most* of the time the exchange will be verbal. And continuous. But another lesson from working in the collaborative arts of film, TV and theater is that in acting – *good* acting – *how* a particular line is spoken is often of less importance than how the actor *listens* – and reacts to – what the other players are saying and/or doing. It is one of the reasons why the better TV writers include (when necessary) judicious stage directions (pauses, gestures, emphasis) in their teleplays. Novelists can profit from thinking this way when writing dialogue.

While on the subject, though it has become a convention to refrain from including such directions in stageplays and screenplays (in the latter, largely because of prevailing fantasies such as the *Auteur Theory*) it is one with which I disagree, and ignore.

Writing for the visual media, I try to use the actors as more than just mouthpieces for my dialogue. I try *whenever* I can to suggest – to spell out in my stage directions – *how* they should react — with *body language*, what they should say *without* speaking. And when I write a novel, I do the same thing. Ergo, when I write dialogue, then rewrite it and rewrite it again, one of the final tests to which I subject it is — does this or that really *need* to be said?

Far more often than not, it can use cutting. Fewer words — shorter speeches. More elliptical.

But — I never fail to be amazed by how often *no* words are even *better*.

How often *silence* is more eloquent. How many instances in which the character can convey his or her thoughts more dramatically — or more comically — with a look, a stare, a shudder, averted eyes, or — more actively and obviously, say, a clumsy gesture such as dropping an object or almost knocking over a glass of wine?

A common criticism one hears in TV writers' rooms is that this or that material "reads like a radio script." Meaning: with radio, the writer must communicate *without* picture – with sounds only – most of which are the words spoken by the actors. Conversely, one of the tests of a well-written screenplay, teleplay or stageplay is that, in order for the audience to get it, it should be necessary to *watch* the show as well as hear it.

Comedy, incidentally — is *all* about non-verbal reactions — also referred to as "takes," the way the actors respond to something funny that's just happened. In plays and movie comedies such reactions help to cue the audience that it's okay to laugh, that what they've just seen or heard is funny. And in a theater, the laughter is then supposed to become infectious. Which is one of the reasons TV sitcoms have those often-intrusive laugh-tracks. Typically, the show is going to be viewed in rooms occupied by only one or two people, and the prevailing wisdom (I use the term with tongue *inching* toward cheek) is that such small audiences, not having the luxury of communal laughter afforded by a theater-setting, need additional prodding in order to enjoy the jokes. The other, and perhaps primary reason for laugh-tracks is that most of the material isn't funny. But that's another story.

As authors, we must *write* the silences as part of our dialogue-exchanges. In a sense, it's like being a writer-director in film. The *words* spoken in dialogue are by themselves not enough. Whether teleplay or filmscript or narrative prose — we — the writers — need to *visualize* for the reader — and for ourselves. The gestures, the glances, the reactions that convey the *hearer*'s as well as the speaker's emotional state, communicating the thoughts *behind* the words.

In a real sense it's about:

Helping *Direct* Your Actors' Dialogue

As mentioned, in television scripts we frequently include "parentheticals" (stage directions) above – and sometimes in the middle of – a block of dialogue to ensure that the actor and/or director understands the meaning we want communicated – a flavor or attitude that might not be obvious upon first reading a line of dialogue. Some examples: (ironically), (sarcastically), (with an edge), (wryly), (mutters), (cool), (icy), (choking), (pissed), and so on.

In short-story and novel writing the same thing applies – only more so. I'm astonished by the amount of fiction that I (start to) read, in which the dialogue sequences contain little or no description of what the characters are *doing* while delivering their lines. There's a *lot* more to writing effective dialogue than simply recording the words coming out of a character's mouth. It's sometimes called context. And it means that the writer must *be there* – must truly *imagine* the scene. We *are* the directors. The painters of the picture. Which is not to say we should belabor our physical descriptions, a point that's expanded upon earlier (pages 156, 157).

Nonetheless, imagining – and writing – your characters' physical attitudes (Is this one slumped – or that one leaning forward intently?) and/or gestures (hand, eye, whatever) *while* they're speaking and/or listening – is as essential a part of writing effective dialogue as are the speeches you give them. More about that in *Choreography* (page 153).

Memorable Dialogue

In TV scriptwriting, I'm usually guided by the following: I want my characters to talk less like real-life people speak, and more like real-life people *wish* they spoke.

We've all seen and heard person-on-the-street interviews, or taped conversations containing mostly smalltalk.

They're pretty dull.

And ungrammatical.

And inarticulate.

Lots of "*I'm like youknow...*" and "*I went '.....,' and then he goes...*" and that sort of thing. Lots of "uh's" and "um's."

Do we *ever* want our dialogue to come off that way? Sometimes, absolutely. It can *feel* very authentic. It *says* a great deal about those individuals. It makes for great *character stuff.* We can learn much about dialogue-writing from reading transcripts or listening to such "real" conversations. We just have to train ourselves to use it with restraint, to shape it to *our* needs and storytelling goals, not least *because* our audience, having *chosen* to read or view *fiction*, has *different expectations* than it would had it chosen a factual piece.

Let's consider the character that – as part of who he is, speaks in clichés, in platitudes. Or repeats himself. Both say a lot about the individual. Just be sure that that's what *you* want to say about him.

When we're writing the words that our more articulate, more educated, more *together* characters speak, when we're putting sentences in the mouth of our lawyer-protagonist, or our marine biologist heroine, it's a different ballgame. Do we want them to come off stodgy — or hip? Do we see them as pretentious — or regular guys? Lighthearted or serious? These are some of the important choices we must make when writing dialogue.

And above all – the mandate. Keep it *entertaining*. Which dull, conflict-free transactions are *not*.

Dialect

The keyword here is "*sparingly.*" Expressions such as "runnin'" or "sittin'" are okay, but use them prudently, *and* in character. "Settin'" (for "sitting") is acceptable to make the point that the speaker is, say, rural. But that should be about the limit. Obviously, vernacular, ungrammatical dialogue has its place, and makes a telling statement about the character speaking it. But as with so much of writing, a little can make a big impact. Moreover, no small part of the reason for minimizing dialect is that it's difficult to read.

Crosstalk

Still another lesson we can learn from listening to real conversation is how frequently people do *not* directly answer the words just spoken to them by another person, but rather, respond on some other, apparently unrelated topic. What does it *say* about the responder?

Sometimes, obviously, it's an attempt to change the subject being discussed. Or to *avoid* the subject. Or — it could be a misreading of what was said. Especially effective when employed in a comedic context, it might also indicate self-involvement. Watch almost any episode of *Seinfeld*, which featured four *totally* self-absorbed characters, and you'll be amazed at how much of the dialogue consists of crosstalk, and how well it works in terms of both humor *and* character-delineation.

Applied judiciously in your writing, crosstalk can — along with subtext, or as part of it — make your dialogue sing — make it special.

The Aria

We've all seen and heard arias – used and mostly abused. The moment when the heavy explains himself. But as mentioned, employed prudently, the bad guy's speech about what he stands for – his plan for winning – why he's devoted himself to this or that awful cause – *can* be useful and effective. Particularly if it isn't a "groaner," if it doesn't come off like a speech. And isn't on-the-nose. And is *short*.

And sometimes even heroes need to "say their piece." All those John Wayne Westerns and WWII movies come to mind.

Generally, though, the long-winded aria has overtones of that other problem – the character who knows too much about him-or-herself.

For me, arias are best avoided or, if you find they're necessary, kept brief – so disguised and truncated that they're not *obviously* arias.

Staying *With* It

What you are about to read may come off as a commercial announcement. So be it.

Even if you write historical novels or other period stuff, it is *essential* to stay on top of current trends and events, and *above* all, currently language usage. This is *particularly* true if you wish to write effective contemporary dialogue.

There is *absolutely* no better way to do this than by reading *The New York Times*.

Every day.

Or – more bluntly – if you want to succeed as a writer, you *will* read the New York Times.

Every day

Oh – I've heard the excuses. Too busy, or already swamped with stuff to read.

Forget 'em.

Flat-out – *if you are serious about being a writer – any* kind of writer – reading *The Times* is about as important as your pen, your thesaurus or your word-processor. Now, obviously, very few of us are going to read every word. But you will *invariably* find items of interest and value.

Okay – but – for writing better *dialogue?*

Yes. Sprinkled through *The Times* are contemporary quotes, columns about language and usage – and everything else that's *happening*, from music to the arts to science and technology, to publishing and on and on. You will *absorb* what's going on in the larger world.

The New York Times is, both in breadth of coverage and the quality of its writing, simply The Best In The World. By miles and miles. No other newspaper comes close, and I guarantee that once you become hooked on it, you will become a better writer, not just of dialogue, but of *stories*. Because in *The New York Times* you will *find* stories. I cannot begin to estimate how many of the ideas for the 100 produced television scripts and scores of series and movie pitches I've written were inspired by items I've seen in *The Times* – from book reviews to news stories to obituaries.

Everything in it is better written than *anything* else you will find – anywhere. Further, because the people who produce *The New York Times* take their work *very* seriously – they regard *The Times* as *The Newspaper of Record* – the publication will inform you on subjects and on levels that will amaze you. Not incidentally, it will likely tell you more about what is going on in *your* part of the world than will your local papers. And the blessing is that in all but America's most remote spots, you can receive home delivery of the National Edition seven days per week or, you can access it online. I urge you to do so. It will change you, your perspective *and* your writing. Profoundly.

Tombstoning

In editing a television or film script, one of the things we look for is the accidental repetition of words or phrases. We refer to it as *Tombstoning*, and it's a good thing to avoid, no matter what you're writing. Unless of course, you're doing it intentionally, as in a speech-characteristic, or for emphasis. *All* of us unconsciously repeat words. Computers make Tombstoning easily curable.

Don't Tell Your Audience What it Already Knows

Another of the *cardinal* no-no's that travels well from TV writing to other forms is — do not have your characters (or your narrator) repeat bang-on information about what's already happened in the story, as in the following example: You have played a scene in which we *see* that Evelyn has been murdered. Do not, in the next scene, or several scenes later, nor at *any* time in your story, have one character inform another, "Evelyn was murdered." Refer to the murder, to the deceased, to the details of the case, but do not *repeat* it – *as an item of news* – to your audience or to another character.

Assume that the other characters have been informed. In series TV we usually presuppose, for the purpose of avoiding repetition, that what one of our primary characters learns, another (who was not present) knows by the time he or she next appears.

The lesson here is that it is not only *unnecessary* to play the moment when that second character learns it – it is to be *avoided*.

Now, obviously there will be times when you *want* to illustrate a particular character's reaction to news of something the audience and your other characters know about.

One approach is to *start* the scene just *after* the information has been reported. In the case of Evelyn having been murdered, something on the order of: "Omygod, Evelyn? — I — we saw each other at lunch..." It's even better if the audience *didn't* see them seeing each other at lunch!

Or: "She's — how — how did it happen...?"

Non-repetition applies to details as well. Using Evelyn's murder as an ongoing model, if the cause of death was strangulation, or knife-wound, or gunshot, you only need to *report* it once. Any later allusions should *add* something the audience *doesn't* know.

You get the idea. In TV writing it stems from A) not wasting the viewer's time, and B) not *having* screen-time to waste. It's also about respecting your audience, about not talking down to it. And of course – entertaining.

About the only instance I know of in TV where this was consistently violated was, again, the monumentally successful *Seinfeld*, wherein such repetition was almost a signature of the show. George, for instance, would play a scene at his workplace in which X happened, and then in the next scene, he'd tell Elaine and the others about it. It worked because the casts' *reactions* were so funny — and sometimes the re-telling was funny on its own, with George (or whoever did the re-telling) giving it a particular, possibly distorted spin.

Even so, as a viewer of those *Seinfeld* shows, I used to mentally rewrite the second scene, editing out the re-telling so that we'd see only the reactions. In most cases I believe it would have worked every bit as well, but that is a nitpicky cavil about a truly great show.

It's also an example of *The Writer's Curse*: we're *doomed* to involuntarily "punch-up" nearly every show we see, or book that we read.

Back to telling the audience what it knows, if you *must* do so, give it a fresh angle. But in general, *don't* repeat. Don't waste *your* audience's time, no matter *what* you're writing.

NEVER Write Show-and-Tell Dialogue

We've all seen it done in novels, heard it in movies and TV: "That's it – we've got to tell the Sheriff." Or: "I'm going to the office." And in the next scene, or the one following, the character is – guess what – telling the Sheriff – or at the office. Even if the telling *doesn't* repeat what the audience already knows, *don't tell what a character is going to do, and then show him doing it.* The reasons should be obvious, from loss of surprise to – loss of your audience.

Energy/Urgency

Nothing will keep your audience glued more effectively than high-energy writing. *Active* words. Concise, *essential* descriptions. And *brief,* idiomatic dialogue speeches. Delivered with *urgency.* With *heat.*

Ellen grabbed the phone is far more lively than *Ellen lifted* or *picked up the phone.*

Phil threw the car into gear has more pizzazz than *Phil drove off.*

Scenes that *move,* that advance the story. If it's mostly action rather than talk, even if you're writing something in a pastoral setting, it should have *energy.*

And of course, conflict. Drama. Or the promise of it through platforming.

Bland, pretty pictures are boring.

Further, *nothing* will cause your audience to dial out, stop reading, or switch channels, faster than a *lack* of energy, of urgency, of heat.

Particularly, in your characters and their dialogue.

As mentioned earlier in terms of your characters' goals: if it doesn't matter to *them*, it sure as hell won't matter to your audience.

Awareness of these needs is among the *best* lessons I learned in writing for film and TV – one that *especially* applies to other forms, such as the novel. Much of the energy, the immediacy that is inherent in screenplays is due to the convention of writing stage directions and descriptive passages in *present* tense. The story is unfolding *as* you're reading it – almost as if it's in *real* time. Look at any screen-or-stage-play, and you'll spot it right away. Here's an example:

```
EXT. CENTRAL PARK - MORNING - ALEX


is in sweats, wearing knee-and-elbow pads,
Rollerblading confidently past early-morning joggers,
nannies with prams, looking as if he's simply out for
exercise. As he passes a connecting path, another,
less expert skater falls in unsteadily beside him.
It's Laura; she struggles to maintain his pace.

                    LAURA
         Do you mind - could we slow down?

Alex doesn't slow.
```

Obviously, writing a novel that way, while do-able, would be jarring to the reader. Some novelists and short story writers do employ present tense, and while it apparently works for them, I find it distracting. For me, it's akin to the movie director who's into razzle-dazzle cutting and trick angles, which calls attention to himself – and in the bargain continually reminds me that I'm only watching a movie. When I read narrative prose written in that style (or, for that matter in any *obvious* style), I'm always *aware* of the writer. For the most part, I don't believe that's a good thing – especially if we're trying to immerse our audiences, to cause them to *lose* themselves in our story.

And yet, after so many years of writing scripts, when I decided to try a novel, I was at first frustrated by the convention of composing it in past tense. It seemed to me that it sapped the energy of my sentences. For a brief time I considered using present tense, but rejected it for the reasons mentioned above. Once I got into it, became accustomed to the accepted form, the frustration disappeared. Mostly.

What did not disappear, thankfully, was that extra edge my scriptwriting experience had given me – a heightened awareness of the need to maintain energy and immediacy *despite* the customs of the medium.

Along the way I gained an even greater appreciation of my word processor's grammar-check feature, which *recognizes* sentences written in the passive voice.

Once again, a few movies that illustrate the importance – and effectiveness – of high energy: take a look at *His Girl Friday, Some Like it Hot* (Scr. Billy Wilder and I.A.L. Diamond, based on Robert Thoeren and M. Logan's scr. for the film *Fanfares of Love* – Dir. Billy Wilder); *My Man Godfrey* (Scr. Morrie Ryskind, Eric Hatch and Gregory La Cava, based on Hatch's story, *1101 Park Avenue* – Dir. Gregory La Cava); *The Philadelphia Story* (Scr. Donald Ogden Stewart and Waldo Salt, based on the play by Philip Barry – Dir. George Cukor). All are classic comedies, and they work in part because of the pace of the direction, because the marvelous actors deliver their lines with perfect timing, *and* at machine-gun pace. But they're *written* to be delivered that way. There's no *fat*. The old gangster pictures such as *The Public Enemy* (Scr. Kubec Glasmon, John Bright & Harvey Thew, based on Bright's story, *Beer and Blood* – Dir. William A. Wellman), or *White Heat* (Scr. Ivan Goff, Ben Roberts, based on a story by Virginia Kellogg – Dir. Raoul Walsh), or arguably *the* adventure classic, *Gunga Din* (Scr. Fred Guiol, based on a story by Ben Hecht, Charles MacArthur and William Faulkner, from Rudyard Kipling's poem – Dir. George Stevens), all have that rat-a-tat tempo. Then there's *Mr. Smith Goes to Washington* (Scr. Sidney Buchman, based on Lewis R. Foster's novel, *The Gentleman From Montana* – Dir. Frank Capra), and *Meet John Doe* (Scr. Robert Riskin, based on the story, *The Life and Death of John Doe*, by Robert Presnell and Richard Connell – Dir. Frank Capra) – or anything else Capra directed. These films provide virtually textbook paradigms of this type of high-energy writing, direction and acting. Among the major reasons that they *are* classics.

Frank Capra's delicious memoir, *The Name Above the Title* (from which I learned more about directing than from any of the classes I took), contains a wonderful anecdote about energy and pace that is very relevant to all this.

During the 1940's, the tyrannical Harry Cohn ran Columbia Pictures, where Capra was under contract. Notoriously cheap as well, Cohn ordered that Capra, along with all of the other directors, would be allowed to print no more than *one* take from each camera setup. This was naturally frustrating to the directors, some of whom liked to have as many as eight or nine versions of a scene to choose from in the editing room. Capra's solution was not only brilliant, but markedly changed his style – and his movies – for the better. Capra, who was already one of the best, would call for a shot, the assistant cameraperson would slate it, Capra would call "Action," and the actors would run their lines. *But* instead of calling "Cut!" at the end of the scene, Capra would keep the camera rolling, tell the actors to return – quickly – to their first positions, and run it again – but *faster*. And when they finished that one, he'd have them repeat it, *faster*. Capra would get three or four versions of the scene on his single allowable take. The energy was remarkable, and better yet, the hairdressers and makeup people had no chance to jump in and groom the actors to the high, phony gloss that characterized so many Hollywood movies of the era. The results were amazing, and happily they're still there for all of us to see.

For me as a writer and filmmaker, those pictures — among others — have been my models. For their energy and a *lot* of other stuff. I've learned a lot from them. So will you.

Dialogue Attribution in Prose – An Opinion or Two...

In novels and short stories I've long been struck by what I regard as the rampant, mindless use of "he said," "she said," "said he," etc. I know that many highly regarded and/or successful writers and teachers recommend such usage as a kind of epitome of simplicity. I agree, but *not* in the affirmative sense of "simple."

Why, I wonder, would experienced, quality writers who otherwise (rightly) bust their humps to avoid using clichés, surrender to these without guilt? Or, viewed another way, when does a particular phrase cease being "economical," and morph into a cliché? And how many trees do you suppose they've cost?

To me, even worse is "she asked." Since it so often follows a question mark, the reader *knows* it's a question, right? So why repeat it?

And then there are "he blurted," "she exclaimed," "he queried," etc. If you *must* attribute, rather than committing those atrocities, "he said" begins to look attractive. Almost.

Do I have a solution? Yeah. Work on attribution the way you work on the rest of your writing, with the care you give to your dialogue and your descriptions. Will it make a difference to your readers? Not likely. Will they even be aware of it? Probably not. Especially on a conscious level. *But* – will it make a difference to you as a writer? Emphatically, *yes*. It'll force you to *think*. To challenge yourself about stuff from which most narrative writers take the day off. So that *all* of your writing will become fresher.

It *is* possible, for instance to write an entire novel without employing any of those phrases nor, actually, *any* direct, conventional he-said/she-said attribution – and yet maintain clarity for the reader. I know this because I did it. As I began writing *The Sixteenth Man*, I set that as one of my goals. And I pulled it off. There are probably other examples out there as well, but none that I'm aware of. The important point to me, as with the act of writing the novel, was to see if I could do it.

Oh, the games we play with ourselves...

And, in the process, I found that it contributed to finding my "voice."

There are those who may tell you that as a novelist you "cannot write for the camera," or admonish with similar conceits of literary Puritanism.

They're wrong.

The reader *is* the camera. The reader is *seeing* the pictures. *Imagining* the scene.

Think for a moment about traditional, by-the-numbers dialogue attribution. "She said," does very little to help the reader envision the moment. It says nothing about the body language of the speaker, or her inflection. Was her head cocked to one side? Did her hand, during the speech, touch her face, or did it touch the person to whom she spoke?

Admittedly, noting such detail isn't always important, but when it helps the reader "see" the action, it seems to follow that it will also help the reader "hear" the words. And when the speaker is gesturing to emphasize a point, or is revealing, say, insecurity or anger or even an emotion that contradicts his or her words, *that* is worth communicating to the reader. Again, when a character's response to another's words *isn't* spoken, but is rather a gesture, a look, *that* can be good storytelling.

I think of it as *directing my actors* – just as in my scriptwriting, *describing* when necessary those actions that *augment* their speeches – or – as in non-verbal responses – *replace* them entirely.

SEVEN

CODA

The Rorschach View

The Rorschach-Test Theory-of-The-World is a fundamental and vitally important part of the Writer's Mindset, a way to view what we do as artists that – while arguably defensive/self-protective – is also a very realistic, pragmatic place to be coming from.

In case you're unfamiliar with the term, a "Rorschach Test" (also known as the "Ink Blot Test") is an old psychological examination wherein a subject is shown an irregular two-dimensional shape, usually symmetrically formed by folding a wet inkblot against itself. The blot is *supposed* to be ambiguous, non-representational. The subject is then asked to describe what he or she sees – what the shape looks like. The psychiatrist or psychologist then uses the response – what meaning or image the individual has mentally *projected* onto the inkblot – to help make a judgment about what kind of head-problems this person has.

Well, the longer I'm around, the more convinced I become that the *world* out there, our world, is a gigantic Rorschach Test – that *none* of us are seeing the same thing.

Consider movies, for instance. I do not believe that *any* two people in an audience are seeing the same film. The same is true of how we regard paintings, automobiles, political candidates, sunsets, friends, lovers, children, you-name-them – how we process everything we see, hear, touch, taste and smell. Instead, we're *projecting ourselves* – our hang-ups, biases, childhood-memories, mental limitations, attitudes – all of the myriad equipage we've been collecting, which daily we drag with us to the table of life – onto the screen we're watching or the pages of the novel we're reading (or writing). Or onto the person we've just met, and so on.

All of which is then *reflected* back into our eyes, and translated by our brain.

And *altered* by it.

Filtered through our own personal *stuff*. Not because we ourselves are *necessarily* head-cases, but because *no two of us are identical*, the reflection thrown back at *each* of us is *different*.

Which is why, as artists, we *must* trust *our own* view of the world, our own creative instincts, our own filters. Because the simple of it is that none of us – not you – not I – can possibly insure that *everyone* is going to read into our art what we intended, see it as we would *like* it to be seen.

Correction: It is unlikely that *any*one else is going to *get it* exactly the way you've tried to put it down. The way *you* think it reads. Parts of it – maybe. All of it – almost never. Now, that is an extreme view, but it contains enough truth to be valid.

Am I saying, therefore, that we shouldn't *try* to say what we want to say, the way we want to say it?

Of course not. The intent of this entire book has been to suggest ways to accomplish that. Techniques for effectively manipulating an audience's emotions, grabbing readers and/or viewers by the throat and *making* them *get* what we want them to get. The essence of what I'm trying to say here is this: though I've tried to list as many as I can – there are *very* few surefire ways to make a particular point.

Which is why, finally, I'd like to repeat – and then expand upon – a thought that's of the *utmost* importance. *Believe in yourself – and in your material* — in what you're creating. *Feel* the passion – because if you don't infuse it into your writing, your readers definitely *won't* feel it.

Further, as writers, or any other kind of artist, we *cannot, must not* be supplicants. We cannot go around thrusting our work at others, asking, "What do *you* think? How do *you* like it?" In part because of the truism that your art is *not* going to appeal to everyone. But more than that, because the comments of others will *nearly always* be colored by their tastes and views and biases. And if you listen to too many uninformed or partially informed people, and change your art to suit them, you *will* fail.

I realize that that kind of confidence – that level of self-assurance – is rare for beginners. Hell, I know professional writers who *never* acquire it. Others have it, but without deserving it. But most of us, through the experience – the process – of writing – and writing – and writing – *do* get to that place.

There's an adage that a camel is a horse designed by a committee. Good writing is not done by consensus. Art – however minor it may be – is not created that way. Which does not rule out seeking the comments or suggestions of a competent teacher or editor or literary agent, or someone whose judgment you *really* trust to be without undue bias.

Absorbing their views, making changes based upon them, *can* help your work.

Sometimes.

But in the end, *we* are the ones — you — me — who must decide whether our writing, our art, is what *we* want it to be. We must, therefore, consistently ask ourselves *the tough questions* – many of which I've posed in this book.

All of us, no matter how experienced or professional we may be, are vulnerable to rejection and criticism of our work. It's also difficult to avoid reading the put-downs as a rejection of us – of *ourselves*. But that way madness lies. On the other hand, I do not know a single successful professional writer, myself included, whose work has not been rejected more often than it has been praised – or bought. It's the nature of the Beast.

Scary though it may be, we have got to *put it out there*, our writing *(read: ourselves)*, *believing* that we've said what *we* want to say – or have at least come as close as we're able.

Take – or ignore – the inevitable knocks. But – *do not let them* shake your confidence, or worse, destroy you.

Difficult. Yes.

Harder for some than for others.

But know this – at bottom, once you get past the learning of fundamentals, the techniques, the guideposts, writing is – as with any art form – about emotions. *Your* emotions. The unique way *you* process the world around you.

It is ultimately through our emotions that we *connect* with our audience. Moreover, it is why, to function as *any* kind of artist, in *any* medium, you must open yourself to as wide a range of emotions as you can. If you don't – if you aren't willing or able to reach into your-self – sometimes into places you might not *want* to visit – and to invest that into your writing, you and your work won't make that con-nection.

Nor, if you shield yourself from the lows – as in facing up to the inadequacies in your work, will you be able to enjoy the highs.

That is one of life's most basic tradeoffs.

That is the "art" part. Beyond suggesting that we must get out of its way in order to let it happen, I don't believe it's teachable.

Again, this book is about technique. It's intended not as a definitive or particularly authoritative treatment about how to write fiction, but rather to impart as much as possible of the valuable lessons I learned in the process of a career in television, film and the-ater. I've tried to remove some of the mystery from the gags, the checklist-type criteria that you might not already have in your mental file. *Practical, nuts-and-bolts,* non-theoretical ways to help objectify your view of your own writing, to better enable you to *understand* the mechanics of good, effective storytelling. So you can "fix" your work. So that you can approach it more professionally.

It is also my sincere hope that this book has helped clarify for you some of the more daunting aspects of the craft, providing you with some constructive, I-never-looked-at-it-*quite*-that-way approaches that you can "take to the bank." Concrete knowledge, borne of my experience, that has hopefully added to your skills, and again, much *more* importantly, to the *pleasure* you will derive from your writing.

The End

Index

1101 Park Avenue, 187

39 Steps, The, 105

Abel Magwitch, 127

Abrahams, Jim, 66

Alison, Joan, 20

All the President's Men, 70

Allen, Woody, 85, 108, 141

Ambler, Eric, 20, 53

American Beauty, 90

American Hero, 104

And Now, My Love, 49

Andy Sipowicz, 99

Angela's Ashes, 8

Appointment in Samarra, 96

Arkin, Adam, 40

Ashley Wilkes, 87

Asquith, Anthony, 13

Austen, Jane, 141

Babcock, Barbara, 23

Ball, Alan, 90

Ball, Lucille, 139, 143

Barnum, P.T., 107

Barry, Philip, 187

Barthelme, Donald, 13

Bass, Ron, 138

Baumes, W.L., 20

Beaches, 167

Beauty and the Beast, 63

Beckett, Samuel, 13, 44

Beer and Blood, 187

Beethoven, Ludwig von, 32

Before the Fact, 121

Being John Malkovich, 13

Beinhart, Larry, 104

Benchley, Peter, 126

Bennett, Charles, 105

Berger, Thomas, 87

Bergman, Ingmar, 40, 141

Bernstein, Carl, 70, 104

Billy Budd, 16

Biro, Lajos, 48

Blanche DuBois, 90

Block, Lawrence, 74

Bochco, Steven, 73

Bogart, Humphrey, 86

Bolt, Robert, 97

Brackett, Charles, 48

Brando, Marlon, 35, 36, 86

Bridges, James, 70
Bright, John, 187
Brigid O'Shaughnessy, 12
Bronte, Emily, 114
Brooks, Mel, 13, 127
Buchan, John, 105
Buchman, Sidney, 187
Build My Gallows High, 48
Burnett, Murray, 20
Butch Cassidy and the Sundance Kid, 165
Cabot Cove, 19
Cain, James M., 48
Cannell, Steve, 51
Capra, Frank, 187, 188
Captain Ahab, 95, 96
Carrey, Jim, 143
Carroll, Sidney, 95
Carter, Forrest, 41
Casablanca, 10, 19, 29, 88, 167
Cats, 90
CBS, 21, 71, 100-101
Cervantes, Miguel de, 96
Chandler, Raymond, 11
Chaplin, Charles, 141, 143
Charlie Callan, 50, 108
Chase, David, 100, 114
Chekhov, Anton, 50, 57
Chernus, Sonia, 41
Chertok, Jack, 174
China Syndrome, The, 70-71
Christie, Agatha, 11, 12, 74
Christmas in July, 78, 163
Cinderella, 13
Cinema Paradiso, 40, 41

Clarice Starling, 102
Cody's War, 100
Cohn, Harry, 140, 188
Collector, The, 66
Columbia Pictures, 188
Columbine High School, 20
Columbo, 103
Condon, Richard, 126, 144-145, 158
Connell, Richard, 188
Connery, Sean, 86
Cook, T.S., 70
Cooper, Gary, 86
Coppola, Francis Ford, 165
Corea, Nick, 71
Cotten, Joseph, 53-54
Crime and Punishment, 6, 126, 151
Crowe, Russell, 41
Cruise, Tom, 86
Cukor, George, 13, 187
Cummings, Robert, 72
Curtiz, Michael, 20
Cusack, John, 13
Dahl, John, 69
Dahl, Rick, 69
Dalrymple, Ian, 13
Dart, Iris Rainer, 167
Darth Vader, 103
David vs. Goliath, 63
David, Larry, 107
Davis, Andrew, 102
Dead to Rights, 122
Death of a Salesman, 90
Degas, Edgar, 42, 141
Demme, Jonathan, 102
Diamond, I.A.L., 187

Diaz, Cameron, 138-139
Dickens, Charles, 127
Disneyland, 89
Don Corleone, 100
Don Quixote, 96
Donoghue, Mary Agnes, 167
Dortmunder, 74
Dostoevsky, Fyodor, 6, 141, 151
Douglas, Michael, 86
Doyle, Arthur Conan, 11
Dracula, 100
Dukes of Hazzard, The, 104
DuMaurier, Daphne, 114
Dunaway, Don Carlos, 21
East of Eden, 16
Eastwood, Clint, 41
Eddie Felson, 95-96
Edwards, Blake, 143
Elaine Benes, 184
Eleanor McGinnis, 23-24
Eliot, T.S., 90
Epstein, Julius J., 20
Epstein, Philip G., 20
Everybody Goes to Rick's, 20
Falk, Peter, 103
Fanfares of Love, 187
Faulkner, William, 187
FDR, 111
Fellini, Federico, 40
Fenton, Frank, 48
Film Noir, 12, 47-48
Fischer, Peter, 12, 23
Fitzgerald, F. Scott, 6, 141, 157, 164, 165
Five Graves to Cairo, 48
Fleming, Ian, 103
Jessica Fletcher, 19, 74-75, 122,
148-149
Flynn, Errol, 86
Fonda, Jane, 71
Fontaine, Joan, 121-122
Ford, John, 57
Foster, Lewis R., 187
Foster, Norman, 53
Fowles, John, 66
Frankenstein, 10, 122
Franz, Dennis, 99
Franzoni, David, 41
Friedman, Bruce Jay, 168
Front Page, The, 77
Fugitive, The, 102, 167
Gardner, Erle Stanley, 15
Gavilan, 71-72, 74
George Costanza, 107
Gibson, Mel, 86
Gilbert and Sullivan, 42
Gilligan's Island, 40
Gladiator, 41
Godfather, The, 100, 114, 165
Goff, Ivan, 187
Goldberg, Leonard, 73
Goldman, William, 6, 70, 105, 159, 165, 171
Goldwyn. Sam, 140
Gone to Texas, 41
Gone With the Wind, 87, 151
Gottlieb, Carl, 126
Grady, James, 106
Grant, Cary, 72, 121-122
Grapes of Wrath, The, 168
Gray, Mike, 70
Great Expectations, 127
Great Gatsby, The, 164
Greenwood, Edwin, 105

Greer, Jane, 48
Gregor Samsa, 165
Guiol, Fred, 187
Gunga Din, 187
Guthrie, A.B., Jr., 88
Hamlet, 10
Hammett, Dashiell, 11, 12, 47, 74, 96, 114, 171
Hannibal Lecter, 102
Harris, Thomas, 102, 122
Harrison, Joan, 105, 121
Harry McGraw, 23-24, 57-58, 94
Hatch, Eric, 187
Havelock-Allan, Anthony, 127
Hawks, Howard, 57, 77
Hay, Ian, 105
Heartbreak Kid, The, 168
Hecht, Ben, 77, 187
Hellman, Lillian, 171
Henkin, Hilary, 104
Hercule Poirot, *11*
Hickey, 44
Hill, George Roy, 165
Hilton, James, 20
His Girl Friday, 77, 165, 187
Hitchcock, Alfred, 4-5, 56, 57, 72, 105, 121, 122
Hitler, Adolph, 108
Hogan, P.J., 138
Holt, Will, 110-111
Homes, Geoffrey, 48
Hoover, J. Edgar, 112
Hotel Imperial, 48
Howard, Leslie, 13
Howitt, Peter, 13
Huggins, Roy, 102
Hugo, Victor, 102

Hustler, The, 95
Huston, John, 12
I Love Lucy, 137-139, 143
Iceman Cometh, The, 44
Il Postino, 40
Iles, Frances, 121
Ilsa, 167
Inspector Clouseau, 143
Inspector Javert, 102
Isaacs, Susan, 108, 148
JACK, 111
Jack and the Beanstalk, 103
James Bond, 103, 172
Jane Eyre, 114
Jaws, 126, 152
Jekyll and Hyde, 63
Jessica Novack, 71
JFK, 77, 110-113
Johnson, Malcom, 35
Jonze, Spike, 13
Joubert, 173
Journey Into Fear, 20-21, 53-54, 127
Julian English, 95-96
Kafka, Franz, 13, 165
Kasdan, Lawrence, 165
Kaufman, Charlie, 13
Kaufman, Philip, 41, 165
Kaz, 21
Kazan, Elia, 35-36
Keller, 74
Kellogg, Virginia, 187
Kennedy, John F., 46, 110-113
Kennedy, Joseph P., Jr., 110-113
Kennedy, Joseph P., Sr., 111-113
Kennedy, Rose, 113
Khouri, Callie, 171

King, Stephen, 14, 136
Kipling, Rudyard, 187
Koch, Howard, 20
Kramer, 159
La Cava, Gregory, 187
Lansbury, Angela, 74, 103, 122
Lansbury, Bruce, 103
Launer, Dale, 66
Laurel & Hardy, 143
Law & Harry McGraw, The, 23, 94
Law & Order, 73
Lawton, J.F., 13
Lean, David, 127
Lederer, Charles, 77
Lehman, Ernest , 105
Lelouch, Claude, 40, 49, 141
Leonard, Elmore, 102, 164, 171
Leoncavallo, Ruggero, 20
Lerner, Alan Jay, 13
Les Miserables, 102
Levinson, Barry, 104
Levinson, Richard, 12, 103
Lewis, Cecil, 13
Liebman, Ron, 21
Lieutenant Gerard, 102
Life and Death of John Doe The,
   188
Lily White, 108, 148
Lincoln, Abraham, 61
Link, William, 12, 103
Lipscomb, W.P., 13
Lloyd, Harold, 143
Loewe, Frederick, 13
Logan, John, 41
Logan, M., 187
Loos, Anita, 171
Lost Horizon, 20-21

Love Boat, The, 20
Love Boats, The, 20
Lubitsch, Ernst, 77
Lucas, George, 165
Lucy Riccardo, 137-139, 143
Ludwig, Jerry, 71
MacArthur, Charles, 77, 187
Major Strasser, 167
Malkovich, John, 13
Maltese Falcon, The, 10-12, 47, 96
Mamet, David, 104
Man For All Seasons, A, 97
Man Who Knew Too Much, The,
   105
Manchurian Candidate, The, 126,
   144, 158
Mankiewicz, Joe, 171
Mann, Thomas, 12
Marathon Man, 105
Marshall, Garry, 13, 167
Marston, Dr. William Moulton,
   103
Martin, Steve, 143
Marx Brothers, 143
May, Elaine, 168
Mayer, Louis B., 73, 140
McCourt, Frank, 8
McGivern, Cecil, 127
McQueen, Steve, 86, 88
Meet John Doe, 187
Melanie, 87
Melville, Herman, 16, 95, 96, 165
Mendes, Sam, 90
Mercedes Benz, 98, 101
Metamorphosis, The, 13, 165
Michael Corleone, 100
Michelangelo, 141

Midler, Bette, 66, 166

Milch, David, 73

Miles Archer, 11

Miller, Arthur, 90, 95

Minnesota Fats, 95

Miracle of Morgan's Creek, The, 78

Miss Marple, 11, 74

Mitchell, Margaret, 87, 151

Mitchum, Robert, 48

Moby Dick, 165

Mona Lisa, 126

Monty Python, 143

More, Thomas, 97

Mr. Smith Goes to Washington, 187

Mulroney, Dermot, 138, 139

Murder, She Wrote, 12, 19-20, 52, 67, 74, 122, 134, 148

Murphy, Eddie, 143

Muzhi-muzhi, 93

My Best Friend's Wedding, 138-139

My Fair Lady, 13

My Favorite Martian, 174

My Man Godfrey, 187

Name Above the Title, The, 188

Natica Jackson, 168

NBC, 73

Neame, Ronald, 127

New York Times, The, 182-183

Newman, Paul, 86, 95

Niccol, Andrew, 13

Nicholson, Jack, 86

Nicholson, William, 41

Nick Charles, 74

Ninth Symphony, 32

Nixon, Richard, 61-62, 70, 96

Nora Charles, 74

North By Northwest, 105

NYPD Blue, 73, 99

O'Hara, John, 95, 96, 168, 171

O'Neill, Eugene, 44

Odets, Clifford, 44, 171

Old Possum's Book of Practical Cats, 90

On the Waterfront, 35

Orbach, Jerry, 23

Out of the Past, 47-48

Outlaw Josie Wales, The, 41

Pagliacci, 19

Pakula, Alan J., 70

Parker, Dorothy, 105, 171

Pavignano, Anna, 40

PBS, 78

Perry Mason, 15, 86

Phantom of the Opera, 10

Philadelphia Story, The, 187

Philip Marlowe, 11, 23, 86

Pink Panther, The, 143

Pinter, Harold, 171

Pip, 127

Pollack, Sydney, 106

Polti, Georges, 11

Presnell, Robert, 188

Pretty Woman, 13

Producers, The, 13

Public Enemy, The, 187

Puccini, Giacomo, 141

Puzo, Mario, 100, 165

Pygmalion, 13

Pynchon, Thomas, 13

Quinn, Anthony, 100

Radford, Michael, 40

Raiders of the Lost Ark, 165

Raphaelson, Samson, 121

Raskolnikov, 151
Rawlinson, A.R., 105
Rayfiel, David, 106
Raymond Shaw, 126
Rebecca, 114
Red Rock West, 69
Redford, Robert, 86
Reville, Alma, 105, 121
Rhett Butler, 87
Rice, Anne, 122
Rich Boy, The, 165
Richard III, 100, 164
Richlin, Maurice, 143
Rick, 20, 88, 167
Ricky Riccardo, 138
Riskin, Robert, 187
Roberts, Ben, 187
Roberts, Julia, 138-140
Rockford Files, The, 51
Rogers & Hammerstein, 114
Rolfe, Sam, 21
Romeo and Juliet, 10, 17, 133
Rorschach Test, 126, 191
Ross, Stanley Ralph, 103
Rossen, Robert, 95
Ruthless People, 66
Ryskind, Morrie, 187
Saboteur, 105
Sackler, Howard, 126
Saint, Eva Marie, 35
Salt, Waldo, 187
Sam Spade, 11, 12, 23, 86, 114
Sammy Glick, 96
Sargent, John Singer, 42
Saunders, Jeraldine, 20
Scarlett O'Hara, 87, 94, 151
Scarpelli, Furio, 40

Scarpelli, Giacomo, 40
Schaefer, Jack, 88
Schlesinger, John, 105
Schulberg, Budd, 35, 96, 171
Schwartz, Sherwood, 40
Scott, Ridley, 41
Scott, Tony, 69
Seinfeld, 107, 159, 181, 184
Seinfeld, Jerry, 107
Sellers, Peter, 143
Selznick, David O., 140
Semple, Lorenzo, Jr., 106
Shakespeare, William, 6,10-12,14,
    17, 95, 100, 133, 164, 171
Shane, 88
Shaver, Helen, 71
Shaw, George Bernard, 13
Shelley, Mary, 122
Sherlock Holmes, 11, 114
Silence of the Lambs, 102
Silverman, Fred, 20
Simon, Neil, 168
Six Days of the Condor, 106
Sixteenth Man, The, 31, 45, 50,
    108, 145, 146, 150, 168, 189
Sleeping Beauty, 13, 64
Sliding Doors, 13
Sneaky People, 87
Some Like it Hot, 187
Sopranos, The, 100, 114, 126
Spielberg, Stephen, 41, 126, 152,
    165
Springtime for Hitler, 13
Stark, Richard, 74
Starr, Kenneth, 104
Steinbeck, John, 16, 168
Stevens, George, 88, 187

Stewart, Donald Ogden, 187
Stewart, Jimmy, 72
Stoker, Bram, 100, 122
Streetcar Named Desire, A, 90
Stuart, Jeb, 102
Sturges, Preston, 77-78, 141, 163
Supertrain, 20-21
Suspicion, 121, 122
Tally, Ted, 102
Tarantino, Quentin, 69
Tevis, Walter, 95
The Gentleman From Montana,
    187-188
Thew, Harvey, 187
Thin Man, The, 74
Thoeren, Robert, 187
Three Days of the Condor, 106,
    168, 173
Tony Soprano, 100
Tornatore, Giuseppe, 40
Tourneur, Jacques, 48
Towne, Robert, 171
Troisi, Massimo, 40
True Romance, 69
Truman Show, The, 13
Turow, Scott, 2
TV Guide, 18
Twohy, David, 102
Urich, Robert, 71
Uytterhoeven, Pierre, 49
Viertel, Peter, 105
von Sydow, Max, 173
Wag the Dog, 104
Waiting for Godot, 44
Waiting for Lefty, 44
Walsh, Kay, 127
Walsh, Raoul, 187

Walston, Ray, 174
Warner, Jack, 140
Watergate, 70
Wayne, John, 181
Webber, Andrew Lloyd, 90
Weir, Peter, 13
Welles, Orson, 53
Wellman, William A., 187
Westlake, Donald, 74, 102, 150
What Makes Sammy Run?, 96
White Heat, 187
Wilder, Billy, 48, 187
Williams, Emlyn, 105
Williams, Tennessee, 90
Willis, Constance, 97
Willy Loman, 90
Wolf, Dick, 73
Wonder Woman, 103
Woodward, Bob, 70, 104
Writers Guild of America, 29, 30
Writing the Blockbuster Novel, 150
Wyle E. Coyote, 104
Wyle, George, 40
Wyndham-Lewis, D.B., 105
Zanuck, Darryl, 140
Zinnemann, Fred, 97
Zucker, David & Jerry, 66
Zuckerman, Albert, 150